ONE LIFE TO GIVE

D0839495

Rick Blaisdell

This book is dedicated to Dave Wells,
the precious brother in Christ
who was the most inspirational to me
to consider going with him
on a short-term missions trip.
It is also dedicated to my greatest encouragers-
my beloved wife Faith and our children.
Every time I left on a missions trip, they faithfully
released their faith that God would care for me
while I was away on these many journeys;
some of which have taken me to some very "risky" places.
Leaving them thousands of miles behind, none of us
as a family ever really knew if we would ever see each
other again in this life. We as a family are forever
thankful for God's unfailing love, care and provision
for us all. We give Him all the praise and glory
for the great things He has done!!

FORWORD

God's Heart, God's Love, God's Compassion: The Walk of One Man-Pastor Rick Blaisdell The Resemblance of Jesus

I had the privilege of typing Pastor Rick's journals with the hope that he would then publish them. When I agreed to do this, I did not know how much typing those journals and seeing the pictures of all that happens when he is in India as well would change my life forever.

I call it a privilege because typing those journals showed me so much. One life given completely to Him, one person willing to say, "Here I am Lord, use me" has brought many people out of the darkness in which they lived both overseas and here in the United States. When He ministered, Jesus met people where they were at, He had compassion for them and for all that they were going through. In the journals, Pastor Rick met those where they were at. He sat on dirt floors, or in dimly lit rooms, and brought those gathered the Word of God. Jesus laid hands on the sick and they were healed. The woman with the issue of blood for twelve years (Mark 5:25-34) believed in what she had heard of Jesus so much that she said "If I can just touch his robe, I will be healed." (NLT). Immediately after touching Jesus' robe she was healed. Further down in this chapter, Jesus tells the woman that it was her FAITH that made her well (Mark 5:34).

In India, Rick taught those who gathered around him about faith in God and after his teaching, they were ready to release their faith and be healed and countless many were. I read of nights that did not end until the early morning hours because Rick took the time to pray for all who wanted prayer individually. One by one they came and received their healing. Then Rick would go to leave for Pastor Sharad's to go to sleep for the night and more people would come for prayer out of nowhere. They had heard of others victories and they wanted the same for themselves.

There was one experience in the journals where I saw God so powerfully. Rick woke up at 3am and was crying uncontrollably. It happened to turn out that three Hindu priests were summoning demons for their festival the following day. When I read this, I was reminded of how Jesus responded to acts of this nature-in tearful prayer to His Father.

The people of India after Rick's first trip there would wait for him with excitement and hope when he returned all of the following years. I saw many times when they greeted him with their tears of love for him and the hugs of their hearts. There were many who felt very much the same anytime Jesus was present in the time the bible was written. Their hearts were full of joy, love for Him, and hope in Him.

Jesus said a lot throughout the Gospels that He was here to carry out the will of his Father. I have heard Rick speak almost all of those very same words in regards to the calling that God has put on his life.

Jesus taught in the synagogues, Pastor Rick taught in home based cell groups and a lot of times in the home of his host pastor, Sharad, or in an open field covered by a tent. People came from miles around to hear Jesus and people walked for miles to hear about Jesus through Rick. To see pictures of the children in India huddled on a mat on a floor around Pastor Rick with their hands held high to the Father really touched my heart. It touched my heart because those children really do have a beautiful chance at life now because the seed of God's Word has been planted inside of them at an early age. They may never have to go through all that their parents went through because they heard about Jesus at such a young age.

There was a young man in one of the trips to India who was possessed by evil spirits. All of the others in the town had ostracized him and stayed clear of him because of demon possession. Not Pastor Rick. He went to this young man, put his arms around him, and through prayer released that young man from the demons that had been tormenting him. He had been cutting himself with stones and was living a life of complete loneliness because of those demons, and through Pastor Rick Jesus brought this man deliverance from those demons. After the young man's deliverance, Pastor Rick then baptized him. This reminded me so much of when Jesus healed the demon-possessed man in Mark 2:21-28.

It is quite a privilege to see the Gospel come alive. That is what touched me the most in typing up these journals-seeing miracles today that happened in bible times.

God's heart, God's love, God's compassion-I see it all of the things that Pastor Rick set out to do on the mission trips. I see it in our church. When he prays for one of us, he puts all other things aside and meets us right where we are at and through his trust in God's will for us and our releasing of our faith in Him, people are healed, delivered, set free, and restored. I am one of them.

Many of us as Christians have a desire of our heart to become like Him and to allow others to see Jesus through us. Pastor Rick having such a close resemblance to all that I read about Jesus gives me hope that it is attainable to be just like Jesus. It seems to me that when we give Jesus all that we are, he makes available to us all that he is, and when that touches your heart, there is no turning back because you no longer desire all of the things you once did. All you desire is to know Jesus more, and more, and more, and to live a life that pleases Him and brings glory to His name.

Typing these journals truly strengthened my belief in my God and the people of India are now a part of my daily prayers. Seeing their victories and healings has inspired me to believe God for my own needs. I also saw how God truly does use those who are willing vessels and are completely yielded and submitted to Him.

It was an honor to type up these journals. I pray now that Rick will get to experience the joy of hearing from the many others that read this book and their testimonies of how it changed their lives as well.

Michelle Lynch-Sept. 2, 2011

ONE LIFE TO GIVE

by Rick Blaisdell

Preface

This book was written to be an inspiration to those who may think that just because they are only one person, "What difference can my life make?" If that is you considering whether or not to read this book, please do. I am not a professional writer and have never written a book before and truthfully, may never write another. But through the constant urging of my wife and many faithful friends, and a very strong inner desire to be an encouragement to others, I would like to tell you about a real miracle.

I was raised in rural Vermont from a very early age of 6 months; (I was born in New Hampshire), and learned early in life how to be a survivor. My family consisted of my parents, two younger sisters, a younger brother, and an older half-brother. My dad was very verbally abusive (you'll never amount to anything, you little s.o.b.'s), and other words that I will not write about. He was provoked to anger very quickly and oftentimes we as children were the victims of some pretty horrific beatings. We were not a particularly close family and moved often because of my dad's work. At the age of 8 years, my mom had had enough, and she left, taking all five of us children with her. My dad came home from work at the end of the week and found an empty house. He called the State Police and they soon had located us in Rhode Island. A divorce soon ensued, and before I knew what was happening, all of us kids were put into separate foster homes, so none of us knew where the others were. A year later, my dad remarried and all of us returned home. My step-mom was a very loving and patient woman, and did her best to make a home again for all of us. My dad continued to be like he always was, and trouble reared again, with the violence and abuse. We lived eight miles from the nearest town on a dirt road, (very common in rural Vermont), and had only cold running water (in the summer, because it froze in the winter). But a nearby brook provided well with an axe to chop through the ice. We had no indoor toilet until I was fourteen years old. (this is not uncommon in rural Vermont). But we did always have two large veggie gardens, chickens, and two pigs for food. My step-mom canned a lot of the food for winter, and we stored the potatoes, squash, and turnips in the dirt cellar. We had no time for boredom; there was always much work to do in the summer when school was out. I walked two miles each way to buy our milk, one gallon at a time, and once in awhile, a farmer would sell us some beef from a cow he had killed.

When high school started, I moved away from home. I worked at a local ski area in the evenings and on weekends. I enjoyed the time away from home and became very independent. High school years passed quickly, and in my senior year, when I had turned 18, I enlisted in the US Air Force in 1964. (The Vietnam War was raging and there was a draft at that time). Some of my classmates enlisted in the Marines and went to Vietnam. One was killed and two came back shot up very badly, and another was seriously affected by Agent Orange, (a chemical defoliant sprayed from our military aircraft in Vietnam, Laos, and Cambodia, stripping the trees of their leaves), to expose the supply routes of the communist soldiers advancing south from China. I enjoyed the four years I served, because once again, I liked the freedom and independence. My last two years were spent in Germany. By then, I had discovered how good the German beer was, and became very frequent in the clubs and bars. The military had built me up well in hand-to-hand combat training, survival training and the pride which came with it was a way of life (just like all the others with me), and I was afraid of nothing. I gradually became addicted to alcohol and got involved with a couple 60's rock bands while still in Germany. When I came back to the States in the summer of 1968, I was honorably discharged. I really didn't know what I even wanted to do, so I just began to do whatever work I could find, and continued to play in several bands. A couple more years passed by and I began to get involved with drugs, starting with pot, and eventually into all the others that I have not room or the need to explain. So now I had the best combination of all (in my own eyes): sex, drugs, and rock and roll. I got married and we both continued this lifestyle for two years, including some time in Florida. While we were living in Hollywood

Florida, I had taken a job for a floor cleaning company that worked at night after businesses were closed. One night, as I was walking home (about 3am), I was apprehended at gunpoint by a man who had pulled up beside me in his car. He ordered me to get in and there was no place to run and no place to hide. He began driving far away from where I wanted to be and I began to plot my escape. I learned how to jump and roll in my survival training and suddenly, it all came back. I opened the passenger door and rolled out of the car at 35 MPH. The driver shot me in the left knee as I escaped. I lay in the ditch and pretended to be dead. He backed up, looked for a few seconds, and then drove off. I didn't even realize I had been shot until I had managed to walk back towards the hospital on the outskirts of the city. A police car pulled up and I was questioned as to why was I out walking that hour of the morning. One of the policemen shined his flashlight all over me and saw the blood running down into my left shoe. They called an ambulance which took me the rest of the way to the hospital, where I was attended to and released a few hours later. That was the beginning of a very difficult time in my life. I could not work, we lost our apartment, we had no food, and no place to live except on the beach with the sand fleas and the police running us off every night. The gunshot wound took a long time to heal, and eventually, I got into the salt water of the ocean and it began to heal much faster. I got a job at a local race track and finally began to get my life back. That marriage ended in divorce as a result of all the drugs, party lifestyle, and no real values that would last. A daughter was born to us at that time and now she is on her 16th year of service in the US Army.

Amazingly, I still wanted to continue life as I always did. I moved back to Vermont and then to New Hampshire. It seems like I was born with one foot in a suitcase, never staying anywhere for very long. I eventually met my current wife (Faith). She was the sister of one of our band's guitar players. She and I also moved to Florida right after marriage in 1977 and lived there for three years. We worked on golf courses where we could smoke pot in the daytime and drink at all the other times. We moved back to Vermont for two years, and then back to Florida. That was the move that would change our destiny for the rest of our lives. My wife's brother, Danny, (the guitar player), had also moved to Florida and was living there when we moved. He was one of our best "party animals."

Sometime over the course of time, Danny became a born-again Christian. Neither of us even knew what that term meant. But we saw a man's life so radically changed that we could not ignore the evidence. We had also grown tired of the drug/alcohol lifestyle and after six years of marriage, we were looking for something better. Danny became the instrument that God used to bring us to an understanding of being born-again. He took my wife to a pastor's home one Saturday morning while I was working at the golf course. The exact date will always be fixed in my head. It was March 19th, 1983. While she was there, she met Jesus and became born-again. At the golf course, at the very same time, I had just finished mowing the tees on the 3rd hole, and while driving my mower down the cart -path, I began to cry uncontrollably. It was so bad I had to stop the mower. I remember how embarrassed I was and concerned that someone would see me like that. (All that pride coming unglued) It took a few minutes to "get myself together" again. I still didn't know what had happened. I finished my work, washed the mower, and went home. Soon after, my wife and Danny came home, and she was crying also. I asked her "Are you crying because you're sad, or because you're happy?" She replied that she had just accepted Jesus as Lord and Savior. Wow, I was jolted to the core, but I remember saying "Good, if you die and go to Heaven, then I want to go with you. I want what you have." Neither of them knew what to tell me, but unknown to me, they had arranged for that pastor to come to our home the upcoming Monday evening at 7pm. That date is also fixed in my head. It was March 21st, 1983. When he showed up with his wife, I went out on the steps and said "Come on in, I'm ready and I don't want to hear no preachin'" In just a very few moments, I was praying with them, and forgiving all in my life who had wronged me, including a church-going uncle who had sexually molested me for many years (and both of my sisters as well), a very mean father, the man who took off with my first wife, the man who shot me, and everyone else I could think of. I renounced all the drugs and alcohol, and the most amazing miracle happened right then and there. I was instantly freed from the drugs and alcohol, and all the hurt, bitterness, anger, and pride, and God poured into me such a new love for others that I never knew existed. I knew at that moment at the age of 35 years, just how seriously my life had been wasted away. After that revelation, I just knew that I wanted to sow as a seed, whatever life I had left to live, into the lives of others.

Faith and I immediately began to come home every night from work and read our new Bibles out loud to each other, (instead of getting stoned), attend every Bible Study we could find during the week, attending really good teaching seminars, and church twice on every Sunday, including the immediate practice of tithing. We went to all our friends and told them what had happened to us, and they were all very shocked. The pastor and his wife spent two years teaching us and getting us involved with ministry, taking us to two of the local prisons with the gospel, and two nursing homes as well. I began a tract ministry at several local laundry mats, and payphone booths. The tracts went quickly and it was exciting to see such a hunger for the Word of God. We had also immediately begun praying for sick and diseased people and seeing God heal so many of them. So many doors of opportunity had been opened to us. My wife and I never wanted any children before we were saved because they would take up all our party time. But God sure changed that. We began to want children and spent many months searching the scriptures about what God had to say about children. When we knew my wife was pregnant, we began reading the Word of God to our first child while he was still in the womb. We learned the importance of speaking the Word over every circumstance in our lives.

We released our simple child-like faith to believe God for his salvation and for a godly wife for our son, even before he was born. Our son was born in Florida and after another six months, we moved back to Vermont. It took awhile to get resettled and find some work, but all the "God-stuff" continued. Faith and I started our own painting business (New Life Painting). When people asked why we called it that, it opened up a door of opportunity to tell them about the new life God had given to us, and that when the paint job was finished, it was like a new life for the house or the rooms we had painted. A daughter came along in a couple more years. We once again had read the Word over her life while in the womb, and believed for her salvation and a godly husband. New doors of ministry opened up, and eventually, the pastor in Florida and his wife also moved back to Vermont. They and we began to do revival meetings running for three days at a time in many of our surrounding towns. In 1986, Renewed Life in Jesus Church was birthed, starting in our living room, then to a large tent, then back to our living room, and finally in the building which we later were able to purchase in 1988. I was ordained into the ministry on

November 18th, 1990 and continued as the Co-Pastor of the church until the Senior Pastor went to be with the Lord in 1998. We closed down our business which had become very successful, and I began serving full-time as the Senior Pastor in his place. During that time, I have seen so many people come to salvation, healed from many sicknesses and diseases, marriages restored, lives so changed by the power of the gospel. People who had no hope are now filled with hope. Lives that were so devastated have been made into something beautiful. Faith and I have personally witnessed, and still do, what God is very willing and capable of doing in the lives of those who are willing to allow Him to do. To keep the record straight, we have also experienced many disappointments and times of discouragement, but never in God.

In March of 1991, my first opportunity to take the gospel to a foreign nation happened. A member of the Full Gospel Businessmen who attended our church invited me to go with him and two other men into Czechoslovakia, Germany, and Austria. The following text of this book is exactly transcribed from the daily journals I have written and kept as a witness and testimony of how God has taken a formally useless drug addict and alcoholic and transformed my life into something more precious and valuable than I ever knew possible. It is also written to give you, the reader, the courage to never give up, never look back, and always be open to God to use you for all the time you have left to serve Him.

Table of Contents

ONE LIFE
TO
GIVE

Chapter One
1991

This is the first short-term missions trip I've ever been invited to participate in. It happened because I was invited by an Elder (Dave Wells) in the church, who has gone on many such journeys in the past. I have never been away from my wife and two young children for any length of time, and it was something to consider before just packing up and heading to Eastern Europe, leaving them all behind. Our family finances were not very good at the time and it was a sacrifice of sorts to take what money we had available and use it to travel on this particular trip. As it turned out, I had no idea at the time the doors of opportunity that would be opened to me. There are four of us: (Dave W., Jim M., Fred E. and myself), going for nearly three weeks. We will be first in Germany, then crossing the border into Czechoslovakia (A formerly Communist nation), then on to Austria, and finally returning to Germany for the flight home to the States.

Monday, May 6th 1991-

Our flight from Boston to Paris left Logan at 8:15pm, and 6 ½ hours later we arrived in Paris at 8:45am **Tuesday May 7th** Paris time (6 hrs. ahead of Boston time.)

We left Paris at 11:35am on a very short flight to Munich, arriving at 12:50pm. We rented a Volkswagen van at the airport. This would be a very suitable and reasonably comfortable vehicle for the four of us, including our luggage. Along the drive to Regen, Germany we stopped to visit the Dachau Concentration Camp Museum and took photos. One could sense the presence of a very heavy spirit of depression and death all over this place. Dark clouds covered the sky, accompanied by a cold wind and light rain. And yet, not far away, sunshine could be seen most every where else. We stayed for 1 ½ hours before continuing on to our first overnight stay. We stayed with the precious and gracious family of Ulrich S. (a long-time friend of Dave's from FGBMFI) in Regen, (a town quite near the Czech border) until Friday midday.

They let us stay in a large cabin, fed us, and washed our laundry. We arrived at about 7:00pm and stayed up 'till 10:30pm. We had not slept since our last night in America on May 5th, so we slept very well this night which was already Tuesday here.

Wednesday, May 8th-

Bright sunshine with morning frost greeted me as I woke up at 6:30am, prayed and read the Bible until 8:00am. Fred, Jim, and Dave slept until about 8:15. Then we went to the main house for breakfast. Lots of good breads, ham, cheese, yogurt, coffee and juice awaited us and we soon enjoyed our first breakfast in Europe. Then we took 300 Czech tracts and drove into several small towns across the border into Czechoslovakia and were well received by the people. We passed out tracts at bus stops, grocery stores, and inside restaurants. People were very eager to take them and read them. We gave out 5 Bibles. We drove into two larger cities and people were not as eager and would not take the tracts. We went to a large public square in Karlovy and the police came and stopped us from passing out any more tracts in their city. But it was already too late. We met a young man from Yugoslavia and he got saved. We invited him to join us for lunch in a small outside café in the square. The police were keeping us under surveillance from the police station 2nd floor along 4 others who watched us from among the people. The fact that we were witnessing in such a public place in a formerly Communist country was a good testimony for Christ. We certainly got noticed in a hurry. When we left to head back to Germany, we picked up a hitchhiker and gave him a tract to read. After he knew we were Christians, he was terrified of us. His eyes bulged out like his head was being squeezed; he shook, and was sweating heavily. He was also very ready to get out in the next town. We had a light supper and then went to our first meeting which was held in a home. This was the home of our German interpreter and they meet every week. These are the things that God did at this meeting:

1. Man healed of curvature of the spine and oval pupils in his eyes made round.
2. Destroyed ulcers and healed liver (man)
3. Healed man of kidney stones and woman saw a beam of light destroy the stones.
4. Delivered woman from the spirit of depression - another woman saw a black bird fly from her- word of knowledge came forth- the bird was a raven, but God said He had slain the raven and it would torment her no more.

5. God healed a woman's leg.
6. God healed woman with a deep cut on her arm.
7. Man received baptism of the Holy Spirit, also delivered him from fear and intimidation, healed him of severe perspiration problem and filled him with great joy.

Jim gave his testimony and I shared blind Bartimeus. There were about 25 people at this meeting. Some had come from another city to join us but they didn't know why they came or even that we were there to minister. Thank you Holy Spirit!!

Thursday, May 9th -

Partly sunny, cool - slept until 8:15am. Jim and I were so fired up after last night's meeting we couldn't go to sleep and we stayed up until 2:30am.

We had breakfast with our host family and then Ulrich took us for a tour of his forestry operations. He has over 1,000 acres of forest to manage and several houses he rents for Christian advances. Then he took us to a museum to see historical farming in Germany. This was very interesting. All the stores were closed today to celebrate Christ's ascension to heaven. (Ascension Day) Even the schools were closed. What a glorious holiday!!

We got back to our cabin mid-afternoon and rested awhile - then supper at 5:30. Ulrich's prayer meeting will be tonight at 7:30. We were welcomed to attend. About 20 people at this meeting. Jim shared his testimony and then we prayed for the people. This is what God did at this meeting:

1. Healed woman with vertebra problems and made her short leg longer to match the other.
2. Healed 2 others of shorter legs. We watched them grow longer right before our eyes. It was a wonderful miracle!!
3. Healed young girl with eye problem.
4. Healed man with ulcerated tooth.
5. Healed man with sore throat.

After this, we had fellowship with the people, something to eat, and came back to our cabin. Tomorrow after breakfast we leave Germany to Prague. We won't be coming back here.

Friday, May 10th-

This is a typical early May morning in Germany, being sunny and cool. I got up at 6:00am, shaved, showered, and had my devotion time before the others got up. We will be having breakfast about 8:30. Then we'll load the van for the 4 ½ hour trip to Prague, Czechoslovakia. We plan to meet Clark (Dave's son) at 4pm and he will take us to where we stay. We arrived in Prague about 1:30pm. I was driving the van. I never drove in such a mess in all my life. Neither Dave nor Fred knew how to find the square where we were to meet Clark. This city is equal in size to Boston. There are trolley cars and buses and the streets are so narrow and winding you must to watch every second where you're going. But God is faithful. People helped us to find our way and it was about 2:30pm when we got to Wenceslas Square. We found an underground parking garage and walked the rest of the way. There are 1,500, 000 people in this city. It was just like we see on TV in Tokyo. You have to keep moving along on the sidewalk or you'll get knocked down. People are shoulder to shoulder, pushing and shoving. Main Street Chester looks like a morgue compared with this.

Every restaurant was full or closed so Dave and I found a cafeteria where we had to stand up to eat, but the food was delicious. It cost us $.75 for the two of us. Fred and Jim didn't want to stand so they wouldn't eat. Fred found a small outside café and so we went after with him for coffee. He wanted to sit and eat. It was so funny because we found 1 table and waited for 30 minutes for the waiter to come and when he did, he said, "We don't serve food here, only coffee, tea, and other drinks". Boy, Fred was some upset! So he bought us all coffee and it cost nearly $6.00. He should have forgotten his pride and ate with us. We had even got dessert and a large glass of lemonade with our lunch!!

Anyhow, we went to our pre-decided meeting place to wait for Clark. We passed out tracts along the way and in the square. People really like them. About 10 min. before 4pm a young man with a topcoat and suit and bag came to us. With the thousands of people all around it was a miracle he knew who to look for. Clark had not arrived yet. This man introduced himself as Vaclav and told us there had been some new plans made for us. He showed us a brand new meeting schedule and are we ever going to be busy!! He told us he would be our navigator for the entire week in Prague. Also, a free apartment for us!! So far, none of us have spent much more than

$75.00 since we left Vermont. The biggest cost is fuel for the van. Vaclav is also with FGBMFI. He took us to his house which is a ten story apartment building like where we are staying. Before that though, another young Czech man arrived, introduced himself as Martin and said he was our interpreter. He speaks English very well. Then Clark came and miraculously has the next 4 days off and said he will do all the driving for us while he is off, so the seven of us went to Vaclav's apartment on the 9th floor, after leaving our stuff at our place on the 3rd floor. The elevators are so bad only 1 person with suitcases at a time or 3 persons with nothing to carry, can ride at one time We met Vaclav's wife sister & brother and had coffee, cake and fellowship then went out for supper about 6:00. We drove all over looking for a place to eat but because there were seven of us and we had no reservations, we couldn't find a restaurant. So we prayed and right away we found a place with only 1 table left. While we were there Vaclav called Martin and invited him to come join us. So soon he came but also brought a man from Austria named Fritz. So now there are ten of us sitting at this table for 4. Fritz has put together meetings in Vienna, Austria for next weekend and into the following week. So we will surely be busy. Fritz is a train engineer and speaks good German and very good English so God really has put the right people in the right place at the right time. After supper (about 9:30), we went street witnessing and passing out tracts. One street craftsman, who does silhouettes with scissors, got saved, and then I prayed for him to receive the baptism in the Holy Spirit. He got so blessed that he made a free silhouette for Fritz just before he got saved and one for me right after. His girlfriend didn't want to even talk about Jesus and she was not able to sell one silhouette. The other man was so busy after he got saved he knew it was God already blessing his work. So many people came by they had to wait in line so we witnessed to them and passed out tracts to them. Amazingly, they all stayed for their silhouettes to be done. We stayed out until about 11:30pm and Dave and Fred were getting tired. These old men get tired easily. (just kidding!) We others could have stayed up a lot longer. They have a busy schedule for us Sat.

Saturday, May 11th-

7:30am and another cloudy, damp, cool morning greeted us. We will have breakfast at Vaclav's, followed by a short tour with Clark, then one meeting, the dinner, and finally another meeting; such a busy day today. After breakfast, Clark drove us into the middle of the city and we walked all over. We went to the American Embassy to see Shirley Temple Black, but she wasn't there, so we'll have to make an appointment to see her. We had lunch in a Russian restaurant and had vegetables for the first time. Every meal has been the same: ham, cheese, and breads. So this was a good change.

The first meeting was very good. Jim shared about new age and then we all prayed for the people. There were about 75-80 people who came, but I don't remember how many salvations and healings. All I know is by the time we had finished praying, the second meeting started and we didn't get a break in between. We did stop for ham and cheeses and continued right on. Fred and I shared our testimonies and the people came up for prayer. By now, the place was packed as the pictures will show. There appeared to be over 125 in attendance. They had bought dinners for 65 but FGBMFI had to buy twice that amount. We each had one. What miracles He does. So we were there continuously from 4:30pm - till 10pm and then had to leave the banquet room. So we all went outside and continued to minister and pass out tracts till about 11:30pm again. In two days, we've gone through a little more than 1,000 tracts. People come up to us and take them to read. The people here are much more receptive to tracts than in America. Tomorrow, we have to get up early. We have a 3 ½ hour drive to Southern Bohemia, almost on the Austrian border. We have two meetings there, stay overnight then back to Prague on Monday late for another meeting there at night.

Sunday, May 12th-

Another cold and rainy morning dampened our hope to see sunshine. We had breakfast at Vaclav's house and left at 8:45am with our Austrian friend Fritz, Vaclav, Clark, and the four of us. (7) We arrived at our next contact person's home near Austria at 11:30am. It was a house full of beautiful Christians waiting for us to come. A brother and sister - Peter and Jana and their parents own this house. There was a greeting line from their porch to the van. We had a delicious lunch with soup, salads, and desserts. The purpose for the meeting there was to establish a new Full Gospel chapter. People from small towns around here came and the chapter was formed. Then we went to a small church for our first meeting. Every seat was taken and people were standing. At right about 6:00pm here, the power of God fell and I've never seen anything like it!! Every single person we prayed for had an instant miracle healing. Backs, necks, spines, all healed instantly. Arthritis and others instantly healed plus 6 people saved. We prayed for so many people that, once again, we had only 7 minutes to go in the van to go to our next meeting in the hotel where we stayed. Once again, every seat was filled and people standing/sitting in the back balcony. All of us shared and then prayed for the people. Four more salvations and many, many healed. Three members of the city council got saved, of which, one was a doctor. There were many doctors in the crowd and a woman who teaches New Age, but they were powerless compared to our Jesus. We were up till 11:30pm ministering continuously from 4:30 with no rest in between.

Monday, May 13th-

We awoke to another cloudy, cold morning, but there is no rain yet. We will go to a public school today and Jim and I will share. Fred will go to the hospital to pray for the sick there.

9:00am - Peter and his sister, Jana met us at the hotel. Fritz and Fred went with Jana to the hospital where she works. All the doctors who were at last night's meeting work at this hospital, and the one who got saved is the Director of all the other doctors and has great authority to make hospital policies. Fritz wanted to pray for a woman who had died in the night, but they wouldn't let him. They had already removed her lungs and other organs as part of an autopsy. But at least they heard Fritz's testimony that Jesus can and has previously raised the dead. Peter, Jim, and I went to the high school and we had an opportunity that may never happen in America. They allowed us to share our testimonies in the classroom of about 50 - 60 students ages14 - 19, pass out Christian literature, tracts, and Bibles. One of the greatest blessings of all was their teacher, publicly before her students, renounced Baha'i practices and asked for a Bible. She said from hearing how Jesus changed our lives, she now knew that Jesus and Christianity was the only true living religion and she wanted it in her life. The next blessing was to see all the kids reading the literature and tracts and raising their hands for a Bible. After this, we all met back at

Peter's parent's house. We had an 11am appointment with the editor of the city newspaper who wanted to interview us. We had prayed with him the night before so he had heard every one of our testimonies and wanted to know more. We also found out there were many members of the local communist party at the meeting. So God really did a marvelous work there. After lunch, we drove two hours to the next town on our itinerary and met with people who had prepared supper for us and set up our meeting. We had been told that many of the city law makers and officials were openly practicing occult and introducing new age to the people, so we prayed and the Holy Spirit said Jim was to have the whole meeting. There were 2 gypsies there who tried to cast a demonic spell on Jim and they were not successful. When they failed, they left very quickly but they had stayed long enough to hear about the saving delivering power of Jesus. No salvations here, but many came for the baptism in the Holy Spirit and for healing. We finished and about 9pm we headed back to Prague 1 ½ hours away. It was good to get back to our apartment. All of us were very tired

.Tuesday, May 14th-

Wow!! What a wonderful surprise: sunny and cool. Praise the Lord!! This is the first day the sun has shined since we got here last Friday. We have a free day today but two more meetings tonight await us here in Prague. We plan to go to the Embassy again and also to pass out tracts on the streets. Well, so much for our plans! God's are much better. At breakfast at 10am, we found out Vaclav had made an 11am appointment for us with the new Deputy Minister of Education in the Czech Government. It was very fruitful. Not only did he listen, but he will apply to the school system and work to get laws passed to keep cults out of the schools. He served us coffee and then he got saved and baptized in the Holy Ghost. Our next appointment was at 2pm with a reporter from Voice, (not the Full Gospel magazine). We took him to lunch with us and he interviewed us. Then we had a meeting at 6:00pm at a large church (400 people) and I shared my testimony, then at 8pm we met with brothers from England who will join us for the rest of the Czech trip. We will be leaving Prague (our last time) at 8:30am after breakfast, journeying on southeast to Brno for the first meeting at 1pm, then another at 5pm in another town close by (Kromerice)

P.S.-The sunshine only lasted 3 hrs. Then clouds, wind, and rain returned for the rest of the day and still now at 10:30pm.

Wednesday, May 15th-

I got up at 5am to pray and shower, and saw the sun shining until 6:30am then the sky quickly turned cloudy with showers soon following. We then had breakfast at Vaclav's. The family from England is precious in the Lord. Their names are Malcolm, his wife Phyllis, son Sam (13), daughter Holly (11). They all sing and 2 (father and son) play guitars. So now there are ten of us traveling together. We arrived in Brno at 12:40pm for only a lunch meeting with F.G.B.M.F.I. and then to Kromerice. At 5:30pm,we checked into a hotel reserved for us and then spoke at a Full Gospel meeting in the same hotel. The meeting structure was much like those in the U.S. There were nearly 100 people in attendance there. Eight of us shared a short testimony and 25 got saved!! Now its 10:30pm again and Dave and I are in our room on the 8th floor and it feels good to finally go to bed.

Thursday, May 16th-

Today is starting as a beautiful sunny cool morning. From our 8th floor window, we can see out over much of this town; kids going to school, people walking or riding bikes to work. There are not many cars on the back streets. Today is a free day until the meeting back in Brno tonight, so it will be interesting to see what else happens for us today. We'll all be having breakfast at 8:30 and then, who knows? We headed back to Brno at about 12:20pm, called home (yes, I actually called to Vermont) and it was sure nice to hear Bethany and Jeremiah and Faith. Then we had lunch and met with the people who were putting on the meeting. The meeting began at 6pm so we had some time to visit and walk around and have supper. There were about 110 people at this meeting. All of us shared a brief testimony; then Jim spoke on the subject of New Age. Five people received salvation, one received the baptism of the Holy Spirit, and many came for healing and received. Some were healed when we prayed, even without a translator. Thank you Jesus!! The four of us stayed in a private home in one room. We didn't sleep well because of much snoring. But we can't help that.

Friday, May 17th-

We had an early breakfast and met with our English friends who also stayed in a home and we walked and shopped and passed out tracts till it began to rain around 11:30am. We met at 12:30pm with our Czech friend Vaclav and Austrian friend Fritz at a restaurant for lunch and then we drove south to Bratislava, (close to Austria). We spoke at a F.G.B.M.F.I chapter meeting and Fred and I shared testimony and then we had a nice supper about 7:30pm and discussed where all of us will stay and where we minister Saturday. Vaclav, Jim, and I are staying together in one home till Sunday noon. We will both share at 2 meetings on Saturday afternoon and evening, and again in a Baptist church on Sunday morning. Then we cross the border and drive on into Vienna, Austria.

Saturday, May 18th-

Another cloudy, cold, rainy and windy morning awaits us. I've not seen so many days of cold and rain like this. We have experienced only one nice sunny day since we left Germany on May 10th. Jim and I had a nice morning off which we spent here with Sam (one son who understands and speaks very good English). We had lunch and then went to the meeting hall. The first meeting was at 3pm and once again, there were so many people to pray for, we ministered right into the start of the 2nd meeting at 6pm. The place was packed, with standing room only. The Holy Spirit moved mightily and many were saved and healed and most of the Baptist Church members who attended came forward to receive the baptism of Holy Spirit!! We were blessed with a nice supper during the second meeting also. It was about 10pm when we left so it was another long time of ministering to these precious people.

Sunday May 19th-

It's now 6:30am, and still cold, windy and rainy. Today Jim and I will be at the Baptist Church. They have a Spirit-filled powerful youth group of about 70 teenagers on fire for Jesus!! Most were at the meeting last night. They experience much persecution and opposition from the other Baptists in the congregation and there is a big split coming in this church. They have a young Pastor fresh out of seminary school who openly teaches against the baptism of the Holy Spirit;

but we prayed for him that God will show him it is real and for today. When we got to the church, the Pastor had changed his mind about letting us speak. Jim got five minutes and I got none. I know the Pastor didn't want us to tell the people about all the miracles Jesus did for us. And then he did his anti-Holy Spirit teaching. We know because our translator was with us. After the service, many of the people came to us and apologized for the Pastor not letting us speak. But we tried to encourage them to keep praying for him and to not let strife and division cause hate or bitterness towards him, and to seek God for what direction He would have them to go. Also we had a tremendous wind storm this morning and tree limbs were scattered everywhere. Bricks were blown from buildings and some fell on our translator's car. The bricks smashed the windshield and put a huge dent in the hood. Jim and I gave her some money to help toward repair costs. We know this was Satan trying to get back at us for all the souls saved and people healed.

We all met for lunch at 12:20pm and then drove west to Vienna, Austria. As soon as we got to the border, the clouds began to break and by the time we got to Vienna, the sun was shining brightly and it was warmer. We first went to Fritz's house, and then he drove us to a high mountain overlooking the city and the famous Danube River. It was beautiful. It really is blue. Then we went to church where we were taken in by an English family for the next 2 days. They have a large modern house with many rooms to take in travelers. This is their ministry. We will be here till Wednesday.

Monday, May 20th-

At last, a beautiful blue sky and sunshine greets us this morning!! After today, we have no more scheduled meetings. The Lord has given us direction that we are to rest and see the glory of His creation. So now we'll be tourists. Praise the Lord!! I stayed here after breakfast just to pray and read and relax. At 12 noon Fritz's family came and Malcolm's family came and all of us had lunch together. Then some of us went to a local vineyard. It was very beautiful there, I took my small bible and read John 15:1-8 there and took lots of pictures. By the time we got back to the house, it was time to go to one last F.G.B.M.F.I. meeting and dinner. Dave and I shared our testimonies, followed by Malcolm, Jim, and Fred. It was a very special time because this was the last time we were all together. Malcolm heads back to Prague in the morning (Tues.), we'll see Fritz in America in mid June, and we're leaving here at about 8am after breakfast.

Tuesday, May 21st- (Oh Yea, it's my birthday! #45)

We rose early to find a cool, partly cloudy but dry morning. After breakfast, we loaded the van, got some money exchanged at a bank and began our trip west through Austria. We stopped in Salzburg where "The Sound of Music" was filmed. We went through the huge castle there and saw some of the city. We ate lunch at about 3pm high up in the castle overlooking the Austrian side of the Alps. Absolutely breathtaking beauty!! We then continued west to a small town called Bad Tolz, Germany where we spent the night in a hotel. From the outside patio café you could look right across to see the Alps again. Breakfast was a real treat. Buffet style with lots of fruit, cereals, breads, eggs, juice, so we stuffed ourselves. It came with our room rents so we didn't want to pass it up.

Wednesday, May 22nd-

A refreshing sunny, cool mountainous morning greeted us. After breakfast, we continued west along the northern side of the Alps in southern Germany. Dave wanted us to see the small town of Oberammergau where a live Passion Play of Jesus is done every 10 years. The last time was 1990 so we missed it but we walked around the town and then drove more into the Alps to the town of Neuschwanstein to visit King Ludwig II's castle. It took about 3 hours to go through it and then a light lunch. Then we drove north to Munich to the airport to return the van. We ate supper at a McDonald's after taking a taxi into town from the airport. We stayed at a hotel and went to bed early.

Thursday, May 23rd-

It's sunny, cool, and we are all excited to be flying back to America today. We got up at 4:30 am. We had very little time left, but we did have a very quick light, breakfast at 5am. The taxi came for us at 5:25am. to take us to Munich Airport. We flew out at 8 am. arriving in Paris at 9:30 am. We then left Paris at 12:15pm Europe time, and flew non - stop to Boston arriving at 1:10pm Boston time. Christian couldn't find us until nearly 3pm so we didn't get home until almost

7pm.because of so much traffic in Boston and we also stopped in Keene for supper.

END OF TRIP!!

Chapter Two
1992

This journey is the result of last year's many invitations to return, including some by mail. After much prayer and fasting, I received peace about going again and visiting and ministering in many of the same cities and villages where I went with Dave W.

I also wanted to bring a younger new believer with me (Karl E.) who had a burning heart for evangelism. He agreed to go with me, and the process of releasing our faith together for all the journey's needs began. Fred E. from last year's team was also flying to Vienna on his way to the Baltic States of Latvia, Estonia, and Lithuania (northwestern Russian states along the Baltic Sea) for a ministry trip also. We had agreed to meet him in Prague. It was several months before we had been provided with enough money for our plane tickets and for the month-long time we would be in Europe. At last, the day has arrived for our departure.

Sunday, Apr. 12th-Vienna, Austria

Dave W. drove Karl and I to Logan Airport in Boston for our flight to Vienna. We arrived right on time, 12:15pm local Austria time, stayed up all afternoon, including lunch at a Chinese restaurant, then a drive through the city. A little later, we had a nice lengthy, prayer walk. We encountered a group of Satanists and spoke the Name of Jesus over them, causing them to flee. We also had the opportunity to lay hands on a beggar at a Catholic church. In the evening, we went to church at Vienna International where we witnessed 17 salvations after hearing the message brought by a pastor from Sri Lanka, Ceylon (an island off the southeast coast of India). Later, we came back to Fritz's flat and stayed up until 11:30pm, making it 36 hours since we had last slept back in the U.S.

Monday, Apr. 13th-

We slept very well and got up at 8am, showered, packed, had breakfast, and drove to Prague, Czechoslovakia to meet with Vaclav and others to discuss the plan of travel for the ministry.

Tuesday, Apr. 14th- Prague

Fred E. arrived right on time at the Prague Airport at 10:15am. Our first appointment was at 4:30pm with the Director of Czech International Bible Society

Our first official meeting was a 6pm New Age Seminar in North Prague. 350 to 375 people attended. After the seminar, we went to Harvest International and had fellowship with them and ate. We also met some people from Christ is the Answer Ministries. They have the benches from Reinhard Bonnke's 10,000 people tent. Both of these ministries are tent ministries and travel throughout the Czech Republic and Slovakia. (Both are now officially two separate states, (Prague being the capital of Czech Republic, and Bratislava the capital of the Republic of Slovakia).

Wednesday, Apr. 15th- Prague

We had breakfast at our flat; then went into city to hand out tracts all morning. We had a picnic lunch in park and passed out tracts until meeting time.

The F.G.B.M.I meeting was at 6:30pm with 70-80 people attending. One girl received salvation; another girl was delivered from demons and depression, and we prayed for many more for their healing.

After the meeting ended around at 11pm, we went out to pass out tracts again until 12:30am. We met and ministered to musicians from Sweden, on the Charles Bridge.

Thursday, Apr. 16th- Prague

Breakfast was served at Vaclav's flat at 9:30am. We then returned to the flat we were provided with from a young school teacher named Danielle. We fellowshipped with her and rested until it was time for the meeting in Ukdz.

Karl and I spoke at a new Age Seminar at 5:30pm. Three people were saved and many others were prayed for. The meeting was officially over at 8:30 but Holy Spirit was working powerfully with many people weeping and repenting until the room closed at 10pm.

Friday, Apr. 17th- Pribram

We awoke early to find it snowing heavily and very cold. Peter and Danielle came to the flat and made breakfast for us. We also had Martin's car to drive (Skoda) to drive with Fritz's car.

We left Prague at 1:30pm to be in Pribram at 3pm. for prayer and a light lunch. The Seminar was at 4pm. and the meeting place full. There were about 60 people, including many young in their teens. A powerful outpouring of the Holy Spirit resulted in ten new believers for and one received the baptism of the Holy Spirit. We experienced a kindred spirit of love and family. We were welcomed with great love. We stayed overnight with brethren after this meeting which lasted for five hours. Our friend Milos Popps translated but also shared his testimony.

Saturday, Apr. 18th- Tabor

We were greeted out on the highway by six of the brethren who had walked to meet us as we drove into town. We went to the Pastor's house for short time of fellowship and prayer; then all of us went into town to pass out tracts and witness. We sang Jesus songs right in the center of town and someone was just married there. We sang them songs and prayed blessings upon them and the entire wedding party came to us, took pictures, fellowshipped with us and really enjoyed what we did. Then we went to a restaurant for dinner and then tour next meeting being held at the town movie theatre. Once again, the room was filled to capacity. There were two people saved, and absolutely every person came forward for prayers. Four of us prayed continuously for 11/2 hours until all were prayed for. This meeting also lasted 5 hours. The Holy Spirit fell mightily and many were weeping and rejoicing as two nearly blind people were healed and one deaf person healed. As at the other meetings, most of the people had never known under Communism about the great joy of the Lord. Then we left for the next town and checked into a hotel. Our rooms were very nice, each with a private bathroom and shower for only $10 per night. (Many European hotels have only one bathroom per floor, to be shared with all the other guests on that particular floor.) We will be staying here through Monday night.

**Sunday, Apr. 19th- **Jindriciiuv Hradec

At 10am we went to a girl's Reformatory School. Seven girls were living there and one teacher. After Karl and I shared our testimonies, five of the girls and the teacher got saved - Praise the Lord. We also went to Pocatky to invite a waitress, her brother, and mother to our meeting tomorrow night.

Later at 2pm we were taken to pray for a lady with a brain tumor and led her son and daughter-in-law to Jesus. He was the newspaper reporter who interviewed us last year.

At 6:30pm.we spoke at the FGBMFI chapter meeting with 35 people in attendance. One person received healing for his back and he also received the baptism of the Holy Spirit. There were no new salvations that we were aware of.

**Monday, Apr. 20th- **Pocatky

This is where we went yesterday morning to invite the waitress, her brother and mother to this evening's meeting.

At 12 noon we had lunch with Jana and her parents

At 3pm we were notified that the waitress's father would not allow her and her brother to come because it would be too late when the meeting was over.

At4pm we supper with Peter Jasek

At 6pm we spoke at the FGBMFI Chapter Meeting. There were 33 people including ourselves. 7 unsaved there. All seven saved including the mayor of the city. Got back to hotel at 11:30 pm

**Tuesday, Apr. 21st- **Trebon

10am - leave hotel in Pocatky for Trebon

11am - meet with Karel

12 noon - lunch at Karel's and we will stay with Karel tonight

At 6pm we spoke at the FGBMFI Chapter Meeting. 30 people attended and three got saved. Most were very reluctant to respond due to many years of communist influence, but the Holy Spirit had His way. We witnessed many healings and one miracle healing.

**Wednesday, Apr. 22nd- **Klatovy

At 9am- we left Karel's house after an early breakfast. Karl and I went to a psychiatric hospital to minister to two patients with many occult related problems. Both refused deliverance, but one spoke the names of all eight spirits he called upon for power and told us which ones had more authority than the others. Fritz and Fred's trip to the nursing school was very fruitful, with 40 students receiving the Lord!!

11:30 am - arrived in Klatovy

We met Vaclav, had lunch, and met with people who took us to a hotel where we would be spending the night when the meetings are all finished for the day.

At 5pm, a New Age Meeting was held. Out of the 100 people present, fifteen became born again! It was truly an excellent turnout because only 25 - 30 were expected, but 100 showed up including Ulrich and his family from Germany. Along with the 15 who got saved, many others received the baptism of the Holy Spirit. Many of them were slain in the Spirit. One lady went down before she was even prayed for. She smashed a chair, laid on the floor for awhile, got up, I prayed for her and she was down again. Many slain in the Spirit were still standing because people behind them were holding them up so they could not fall down. God's Spirit moved mightily in this meeting and many were healed and delivered.

**Thursday, Apr. 23rd- **Plzen

This morning we had some free time. At 12 noon we had lunch with our translators and a pastor from Plzen. At 4pm we met in a small church with 40 people, all of them being believers already. My teaching was on "Standing as Christians" against powers of darkness.

At 7pm Karl and I spoke at a meeting held in the Eden cinema.(movie theater). There were 75 people in attendance including 14 unsaved; but not for long. They all received salvation!! The Holy Spirit poured out in waves. There were many people slain in the Spirit and were lying on the floor of the front part of the theater as they responded to the altar call. There were also many, many healings. The meeting lasted till 11pm.

****An interesting note about all the "slain in the Spirit"- none, not one that we knew of, had ever even heard of this experience, and yet we witnessed it so many times whenever we laid hands on the people and prayed for their needs. Some fell backwards, some fell**

forward and landed on us, some fell straight down, and some fell to the side. Many of them laughed, many of them cried, but they all testified that they had experienced something very powerful and wonderful that brought them great joy and peace they had never known before.

Friday, Apr. 24th- As

Today Fritz is leaving for Austria. We shared our testimonies in one classroom and told how most of the public schools are in America without God. A Brother from Plzen drove with us because Fritz is in Vienna. We need two cars for luggage and the five of us. We got here (As) at 2:30pm. A nice, cozy apartment was provided for us. We rested wonderfully because of the long ride and little sleep from last night's late meeting.

At 7pm we spoke at a new chapter of FGBMFI. Out of the 80 people, nine received their salvation as God did it again!! I've never seen anything like it. This has continued night after night. The two of us prayed for so many people we were not finished until 11:30pm. Many of the Beloveds were "slain in the Spirit" and lying on the floor. **Our God is an awesome God!!**

Saturday, Apr. 25th- Sokolov

We had breakfast at 8am, and at 9am, we had a small informal home gathering with the opportunity to minister deliverance to a woman who had been involved with black magic. After we explained to her the seriousness of what she was involved with, she was very quick to renounce it and repent from it. The Lord was just as quick to deliver her from all the problems it had made for her. One girl also received salvation. We then went to visit someone in a hospital and prayed for her healing. Then it was lunch time and the Lord arranged for us to have a Jesus picnic in a park with 17 young Christians.

At 3pm we had a meeting at the World Cinema, with 100 in attendance. Karl and I really loved these meetings in a movie theater because when we had an altar call, we could hear the old wooden seats snap upright with a loud slapping sound all over the theater. Eight people got saved and one of the eight was the #1Yoga teacher in this city. We couldn't help but think of how much influence this new believer would have on all her followers!!

At 6pm we held another New age Seminar. 50 people came, but there were no new salvations tonight. There was one person who received healing after prayer.

Sunday, Apr. 26th- Decin

9am presented us with an opportunity to teach on communion in a Baptist church and Karl and I then served the elements to the congregation.

At 4pm we had a "New Life" meeting at another church with about 30 people in attendance. Three received salvation. The Spirit of God really poured out love and healing here. Many of these churches are small in size because of all the formerly communist persecution for seventy years and many of the believers were still very much not sure if it was safe to gather publicly yet A deaf man was also instantly healed at this meeting!!

Monday, Apr. 27th- Usti to Litomerice –

We went into town and passed out 200 tracts!!! The people were very receptive to read them in their own language. In the afternoon we departed for Litomerice.

At 6pm we both spoke at another new chapter of FGBMFI. At this particular meeting there were 22 people consisting mostly of doctors and medical students. There was much outward doubt and unbelief among them about the things of God, but there was one salvation and three others baptized in the Holy Spirit.

Tuesday, Apr. 28th- Prague

We ministered to a young man who has followed us for four days by train. He needs much follow-up and prayer.

We had an early supper at Vaclav's flat and right after, Milos left to return to Harvest International.

Karl and I came to Danielle's flat. She is a school teacher and she allowed us to stay at her flat while she stayed at her sister's flat. She had more food prepared for us and beds ready. Just like coming home here. We had good fellowship with her and her friends, prayed, praised the Lord and went to bed early - 10pm.

**Wednesday, Apr. 29th- ** Prague

It's now morning and we didn't go anywhere. We prayed, praised and rested. We have just completed the first two weeks of ministry and the longest and most enduring part of our journey is still ahead. Danielle's sister and children came by to see us. We had time to pray and bless them and the new baby in her womb. She said the baby leaped inside her when we laid hands on her and prayed. The afternoon was more of the same. Peter and Danielle came home from work so we had more good fellowship. At 5pm we had supper at Vaclav's apartment. Fritz returned from Vienna and joined with us again.

At 7pm we were invited to attend another small, informal meeting with 22 people. There were three unsaved who had the opportunity to be saved - but did not receive Jesus, but the Holy Spirit still worked in their hearts.

**Thursday, Apr. 30th- ** Pardubice

Fred and Vaclav went into the city. Karl, Fritz and I prayed, praised and fellowshipped and enjoyed our last few hours here in Daniela's flat. Then we had lunch at 12:30 with Vaclav. Then we left beautiful Prague for the last time and travelled east by train to the town of Pardubice.

At 6pm we spoke at another New Age seminar with 40 people in attendance. Two received salvation, including our translator. That was quite exciting!

**Friday, May 1st- ** Hradec Kralove

A two day New Age seminar invited each of us to speak. This meeting was much larger than some of the others with around 500 people in attendance. Our busy ministry schedule allowed us to speak at just the first day's seminar. We each shared our testimony about the changed life found only in a personal relationship with God through Jesus Christ. We left at 1:30pm for the long drive to Ostrava, a city in the far eastern part of the Czech Republic.

We arrived in Ostrava at 8pm. All four of us stayed in same flat which was made available for us. We stayed up late, discussing the meetings scheduled for tomorrow.

Saturday, May 2nd- Ostrava

Our first meeting today was a New Age seminar from 9am to 11am. Fritz and Karl shared their testimonies. 180 people attended. Three people received salvation, one recommitted to Christ, and many received healings.

From 6pm to 9pm, Karl and I shared our testimonies at another meeting. 200 people in attendance and ten received salvation. We witnessed a very powerful move of the Holy Spirit again!! Many were prayed for, as we released our faith together for healing and deliverance of the people. It was a late night for us, but so rewarding. We'll be leaving early in the morning for our trek southwestward to the small city of Frydek where we will speak at a church for the Sunday morning service.

Sunday, May 3rd- Frydek

At 9am until 11am, we spoke at the church meeting where 50 people had been waiting for our arrival. Two received salvation. The Holy Spirit came suddenly as a wind, with many of the people testifying of receiving healing. From 12 noon to 2pm, we had lunch with the new members of the FGBMFI chapter.

We will enjoy some free time this evening with no meetings scheduled.

Monday, May 4th- Hotel Oskol, Kromeriz

After an early morning breakfast, we continued our southwestern journey to the city of Kromeriz. At 6pm, Malcolm and his team joined us from England. Now we are a team of eight. We will remain joined together for the next portion of the ministry journey. We all shared short testimonies with one new salvation resulting. Many of the people were reluctant to have prayer during the formal part of the meeting, as this was so new for most of them. After the meeting was dismissed, we did have more prayer time and one of the blessings was that a deaf woman received her hearing!!

Tuesday, May 5th- Kromeriz

We were invited to speak at a local high school this morning, with 30 students attending. After two of us shared our testimony, we were not allowed us to have an altar call, but the Holy Spirit had another way of opening a door of opportunity. The students asked many questions about Jesus, rock music, drugs etc. Then after the meeting, two of the students followed us to the Director's office where both of them received the baptism in the Holy Spirit, after the laying on of hands. Both went down under the power of God right there in front of the Director!!

After lunch, we departed, continuing west through the Czech Republic to the city of Brno. Some of our team spoke at a New Age seminar in the evening. A small group of 50 people attended but it was a very exciting and fruitful meeting for the Kingdom of God. Five people received salvation after the Holy Spirit came very quickly and powerfully. Many more were healed and people fell to the floor one after another as they received the baptism in the Holy Spirit.

Fred and our British team members went to the nearby village of Ho Dinin for a couple of meetings, resulting in 26 people receiving salvation.

Wednesday, May 6th- Brno

All of us had an early breakfast together and a time of prayer. Today is the day Fred will leave us and return to Prague, where he will travel by train to the Baltic States to fulfill the remaining time of his mission trip. At midmorning, Fritz, Karl and I will depart for Vienna Austria for two meetings. We will return to the Czech Republic on Friday, May 8th for the last two meetings for our part of this mission journey. The drive from Brno south and across the border into Austria to Vienna took nearly 5 hours but we arrived refreshed by the Lord and ready for whatever He would have for us.

Our first meeting in **Vienna** was at a small Full Gospel Chapter with ten people, all men, in attendance. We were quickly able to discern that these men were filled with pride, strife and division. They wanted no praise music and had not planned to have any musicians or songs to be sung. But in only a few minutes, a precious Sister in Christ showed up with her guitar, telling us that the Lord had sent her to minister in song and word. As soon as she began to sing, the Holy Spirit released His powerful presence. The words of her songs spoke of the love of God, obedience, repentance, and healing of wounds in the body and mind. Every one of these saved men came forward, as they responded to their need for prayer. Much healing of emotions and repentance took place. The really awesome thing about this particular meeting was that none of the three of us, (Karl, Fritz, and myself), ever got to speak. God simply and gently spoke to the men through our Sister with her anointed music and song lyrics.

The second meeting in **Vienna** was attended by 21 people. They were dealing with many problems between husbands and wives, financial, and other family problems. The Holy Spirit moved mightily and every couple left fresh as newlyweds kissing and holding hands!! Praise the Lord. He showed us His love and compassion again.

Thursday, May 7th- Vienna

Karl and I stayed at Fritz and Monika's apartment overnight after last night's two meetings. We had an awesome Austrian breakfast, a quiet morning of loving fellowship and music as Monika sang and played her piano. We took a walk through some of the streets of Vienna, and sensed the Holy Spirit leading us to a Christian bookstore. After entering the store, the Holy Spirit revealed to us that there was an ungodly cassette in with the other Christian music in one corner of the bookstore. We also sensed that the Holy Spirit was going to do something there very soon. We showed the cassette to the store clerk. He was quite shocked that such a thing would be in the store and unknown to him. We asked him if he would like to receive the baptism of the Holy Spirit. He said he would like that very much and he received immediately and very powerfully. Then we prayed that God would give him discernment and encouragement and left him a very blessed man. We ended our evening with a wonderfully prepared spaghetti dinner and prayer before going to bed.

Friday, May 8th-

We were up early, had breakfast, and at 9:15 am we headed back across the border into the Republic of Slovakia to rejoin with Malcolm in Bratislava., the capital city. We all had lunch together and then an 80 mile journey to Topolcany to speak at a small church meeting. There were no new no salvations, but five people were baptized in the Holy Spirit. We prayed for others for their healing.

Fritz, David, and Geoffrey slept in one of the church member's house tonight. Karl, Malcolm and I slept in the pastor's house. We will meet again tomorrow after breakfast.

Saturday, May 9th-

We all went to the town where Monika is from. The landscape was very beautiful, with lush green mountains like Vermont. We had lunch there high upon a mountain overlooking the town. Also, Malcolm and Maria played guitar and all of us sang and praised the Lord in the streets and handed out Bibles. Our last meeting was wonderful. 30 people came, but 16 got saved (10 were gypsies including one of them who turned in a loaded gun). Then we praised the Lord until 11pm, drove to Bratislava (we left Malcolm's team there), and we came back to Vienna, arriving at 3am. We slept late, rested very well, and then after breakfast, Fritz drove Karl and I back to the Vienna Airport, where we departed right on time for our return flight to Logan Airport in Boston. After we came through baggage claim, Customs and Immigration, we were greeted outside by a smiling Dave Wells. We had a wonderful time of sharing the joys of the journey for the entire 3½ ride back to Vermont.

Chapter Three
1994

Trip to Prague April 18, 1994

On this journey, I had planned to bring a brother (Phil A.) from the church, but at the last moment, (Sunday April 17th), he had some heart problems and could not go. After church, I came home and prayed, asking God for who else might go in Phil's place. Karl E. name came to my mind. He was working on Fischer's Island in Long Island Sound at this time. I called him and asked him about going again with me, and he immediately replied that he would go. We needed to leave on Monday the 18th, and it took some time to change the plane ticket from Phil's name to Karl's name. Actually, most of Monday morning was spent at the travel agency to work out the details. Karl hitchhiked from the island to Bradley Airport in Hartford, Connecticut with just a small back pack and his guitar. I met him at Bradley and we both rejoiced that God had opened a door of opportunity for us to travel again together. We flew down to JFK on the small shuttle flight and soon were on our flight to Prague, stopping and changing planes in Paris.

We arrived at Prague airport at 1:30 pm Prague time. Vaclav met us with Milos (one of our translators and very precious brothers whom we met on the previous 1992 trip) and we came by city bus to Vaclav's flat. There was such a joyful reunion and fellowship. Then after supper, we had a great time of prayer at 8pm for all the meetings and cities for souls to be saved. I also prepared a message to the church at Kutna Hora where2 people received the Lord.

Thursday Apr. 21st-

We visited a local high school at 9am. And we had the blessed opportunity to speak before two different English classes about God/Jesus and how American schools need God and prayer again. Then we had lunch and took a bus to Hradec Kralove one hour away. Later in the evening we had a meeting at the YMCA. God's love manifested/descended as a cloud upon the people. There was much weeping, as God poured out His Spirit, and 3 girls were saved. They could not stop weeping for hours. Then we praised and worshiped until midnight with a converted Muslim and another American who played guitar. We spent the night at the Muslim man's home, had breakfast and he took us to the bus station to catch the bus to Prague again. It was about a 3 1/2 hour ride to Prague, then the subway and another bus which finally brought us to Vaclav's house.

(Somehow, somewhere I lost the journal pages for the remainder of this journey)

I deeply apologize to the readers because I do not want to write just from memory, without the journal to verify the meetings and testimony of the wonderful ministry we witnessed the Lord do.

Chapter Four
1996

Prophesies Concerning the Trip- 1996

1. Do not attempt to make things happen on your own. I have gone before you and prepared the way. Work in my Spirit and you will see what I have prepared.

2. Wherever you preach, a standard will be established. This standard will not be removed, even after you are gone. The door will close to many, but to you, it will always be open.

3. Be prepared to go to an unexpected place and do unexpected things.

*fulfilled with Fritz/ Bratislava to Vienna Saturday 3/30

4. Your church will receive a 7-fold return on the fruit produced in Czech/Slovakia.

Scripture
1. Romans 1:8-12
2. Joshua 1:9

Visions – 1996
1. A partially closed/open door with an elbow- (God's?) holding against the door.
2. You will go and when your plane returns, your seat will be empty.*
3. Your arms around a large basket of fruit. This vision was fulfilled at a homeless shelter when I put my arms around large basket of bread and blessed it. Also this night 100 people got saved.
* Similar to Agabus's prophesy/vision concerning Paul. See Acts 21:10-14.

March 1996
Saturday, Mar. 16th-
All is ready overseas. Dave and I have received the Plan of Travel for the Czech Republic from Vaclav. He has prepared 21 meetings in the first ten days, ending in Brno. Malcolm and Fritz have organized

the Republic of Slovakia portion and Malcolm will meet us in Brno on March 29. They are such good organizers for us!! Now we pray and wait for our journey date to arrive! We received a great big prayerful send off from the church Sunday as many of our beloveds laid their hands on us, anointed us with oil, and sent us off.

Tuesday, Mar. 19th-

Dave W. and I are very excited about travelling together again. As he goes with me this time, (my 4th trip, and sadly, his last), we spent our driving time to Logan Airport (Boston), reminiscing of our journey together in 1991 (which was my first). We also remarked how God had once again provided for us to travel again by providing our plane tickets at the miraculously low price of $385.35 round trip per person We left from Logan at 6:15pm on Lufthansa Airlines, and arrived in Prague 10:10am Wed. March 20.

Wednesday, Mar. 20th-

After flying all night, we arrived in Prague right on time. (Forgive me for using this as a good opportunity to put in a "plug" for Lufthansa's timely flight). Norm and Ruth S. (Our American missionary friends from Naples Florida, who are staying in Prague, training three young Pastors to minister to the new believers from the last missions trips), took our luggage in their car and we came by metro (subway) with Vaclav. We had a quick lunch, Dave went to bed for a much-needed rest, and I went 2 hours away to our first meeting at 6pm in Kolin. Ten people, including a local pastor, were in attendance as I spoke from Luke 4:18 and Romans 10:13 - 15, anointed their feet with oil, and prayed for all of them. The Lord greatly encouraged them.

Thursday, Mar. 21st-

Dave and I are staying with Norm and Ruth and we experienced much good quality time with Norm and Ruth today. Then we spoke at a meeting at a local junior high school. We were told it would be very difficult to preach in the schools now and that we could not have an altar call. It was a voluntary meeting for the students and the assembly hall was full. When we finished, we dismissed all who wanted to leave. We had question and answer time. Half the students choose to stay. Then we had a salvation invitation - 15 students saved!! All were 11to 13 years old. We were at the school until 5:40 pm talking with them. All the students wanted us to autograph their tracts and literature. This was quite an exciting meeting to say the least! We had no more meetings today, and went into town with Norm and Ruth for supper.

Friday, Mar. 22nd-

Our day began with breakfast, followed by a long train ride north to Karlovy Vary, which was 4 hours away, and then a 1 hour car ride to the town of Kraslice, our final destination. This town is up in the snowy mountains near the East German border. There were four church groups gathered together in one man's house. He used to be a heroin addict and Jesus saved him and set him free. This was a very good meeting with two saved, one baptism in Holy Spirit, five marriages healed, two people delivered from demonic spirits because of their involvement with the occult. There was much more ministry also and this meeting lasted for five hours. Dave and I spent the night here.

Saturday, Mar. 23rd-

We went to bed about 1 am and got up at 6 am for breakfast. Our train back to Prague left at 8:35 and we got back here at 3 pm. We had a quick lunch, shower, change of clothes, and took a bus into town for another meeting. Three gypsies and two other men were saved at this meeting.

Sunday, Mar. 24th-

We had all morning to spend with Norm and Ruth. We had lunch with Vaclav. Dave will minister in a different town this afternoon and I will be at a homeless shelter in Prague to share gospel with these people. Nearly 150-200 people came at 5 pm for supper prepared by local church volunteers. I shared a very short message of hope and a conservative estimate of 100 people raised their hands for Jesus. Then I stayed and helped in the serving line, and after that, I mingled among them and prayed individually for healing etc. This was the most gut-wrenching situation I've ever ministered in, but God was there to care for each of them. I was told this was first salvation invitation given there. (This is where the vision of my arms and basket happened. See beginning of this chapter.) When I came back to America, I told the person of her vision and how it came to pass and she was very encouraged.

Monday, Mar. 25th-

Dave has been getting very tired out, but we did have all day to spend with Norm and Ruth so we took them out for lunch. Now we will leave at 3pm by train to Usti nad Labem for our next meeting at 7:30 pm. Dave's and my personal observation was that this meeting very much lacked any presence of God's power. There was no ministry, no prayer, very young, rich, cocky businessmen, 2 unsaved and both could not see their need for salvation. We left and both of us were sad because we knew our wonderful heavenly Father had so much He wanted to do, but the hardness of hearts prevented Him.

Tuesday, Mar. 26th-

We stayed overnight with a family of 4 children, who graciously cared for us. We had breakfast and caught an 8 am train back to Prague. We had lunch again with Norm and Ruth and tonight will be our last night in Prague. We both spoke at a F.G.B.M.F meeting which was held in a hotel restaurant. We prayed for quite a few people. We also met some people from a radio station in Plzen. They broadcast Christian programming 24hrs. each month. They recorded Dave and I and broadcasted it on their station which reaches about 40% of the Czech Republic- 3 to 4 million people. We also made contact with people who minister to drug addicts and have been asked to come back next summer to minister to them.

Wednesday, Mar. 27th-

Dave and I spent much of the morning with Norm and Ruth, sadly knowing we would not see them again on this journey. Before we came, they were under much oppression and very discouraged. (They came here for a period of three years on the promise of many who said they would support them with the necessary finances, and ultimately had not kept their word to them.) We've been ministering to them and building them up again. Today, Ulrich Schnerbein.(whom we met on my first trip in 1991), came from Regen, Germany to visit with us. We all went to Vaclav's and fellowshipped, had communion together, and lunch. Norm and Ruth's joy is now fully restored and they looked very good. We and they came into Prague city on the metro to the train station to see us off to Kolin. There were many hugs and tears just before the train left the station with us on it. They really wished we didn't have to leave so soon. Milos Popps came also with us to translate. The evening meeting was good here in Kolin. Some of the people were from the same church group I ministered to the day we arrived. One new Christian tonight- Praise the Lord!! We will spend the night with a family from this church. It snowed this morning in Prague but here in Kolin it looks like spring. No snow, some new green grass, and many of the fields are plowed for spring planting.

Thursday, Mar. 28th-

We awoke to a sunny and chilly morning. We had breakfast at 8 am and went into town. Our train to Zdar will leave at 12:50 pm and we will speak there tonight. This church is one Norm and Ruth minster at. Also, Peter Jasek called and he will come. He may give us a ride to Brno tomorrow and if not, we'll go by train. What a wonderful meeting tonight; one salvation, many prayers for many people, and much ministry by the Holy Spirit. Peter Jasek did not come, so I guess we'll be travelling by train in the morning. We will sleep at a pastor's house and fully expect to wake up tomorrow morning well rested for our next leg of the journey.

Friday, Mar. 29th-

Again, we awoke to another cloudy and cold morning. We had breakfast at 8 am and at 9 am, a time of teaching and ministry at our host pastor's house. There were 7 people from Norm's church who came over for this meeting and fellowship. We had a time of prayer and snacks, went to lunch and left on the 2:30 pm train for Brno. Our evening meeting was in a hotel restaurant, so we decided to get a room for the night. This turned out to be a good idea, because Malcolm and Sam drove up along with Fritz. Dave and I had a very good meeting, 5 people saved, and much other ministry besides. We all went out for supper at 9:30 pm and had great fellowship.

Saturday, Mar. 30th-

It was cloudy and cool again this morning. Dave and Malcolm took Malcolm's car and picked up all our suitcases at the train station. We left them there yesterday because we walked to the hotel about 1 mile from the station. Today we will all have breakfast together. Vaclav will leave later today to return to his flat in Prague. Malcolm has organized the remainder of our trip. We'll be driving to Bratislava. (Capital of Republic of Slovakia, and just a bit east of Vienna, Austria)

I'll ride with Fritz and Dave will ride with Malcolm and Sam. We've already heard about the border guards between Czech and Slovakia. They search all through cars and people's luggage. If they find any item they want, they take it. If you want it back, you must pay them money which constitutes an illegal border tax. But we have prayed over everything and believe God will take us through with no problems. (And that is exactly what happened.) Suddenly, a new plan has emerged: Fritz asked if I'd go to Vienna with him because he wanted to talk with me privately. Monika has left him and he hasn't seen her for 3 ½ weeks. So we did spend the day together and came back in time to Bratislava for our scheduled meeting. It very well attended and the gospel was well- received. 4 people received salvation and many others were prayed for. We then drove nearly two hours east to Partizanske, where we spent the night at Malcolm's flat.

Sunday, Mar. 31st-

We attended Malcolm's church this morning. He has a large gypsy population in the congregation. Dave spoke at the morning service and I for the evening service. There was time given for ministry and prayer. Then we, Malcolm, Phyllis, Sam and Holly went out for pizza. It snowed hard tonight.

Monday, Apr. 1st-

This morning was all white outside but most of the snow melted before noon. We will be on our way back to the States this time next week. Our meeting tonight will be in the same building where the European Men's Camp was held in 1994 when Karl and I were here last. Our 5 pm- meeting started and the room quickly filled. There were mostly gypsies and a few people from Malcolm's church. Most of the other locals did not come from the town because they hate the gypsy believers. We had a good meeting nevertheless, and two more gypsies received salvation. Others came for prayer needs.

Tuesday, Apr. 2nd-

We awoke to find it snowing steadily this morning; about 3 inches overnight but not on the roads. The meeting was cancelled tonight because the snowstorm lasted all day. Over a foot has accumulated and it's still snowing. So we stayed home with Malcolm, Phyllis, and the kids and played Bible Trivia and had a really good time of fun and fellowship.

Wednesday, Apr. 3rd-

A new morning greeted us with a cold, rain/snow mix. We very carefully drove to Bratislava and found much snow there; over a foot and still snowing hard. We went to a high school located right beside a Volkswagen factory where workers were selling drugs to the students. We spoke twice; each time to a group of three classes. Ten people in the first group received salvation, including two teachers. In the second group, one student and a teacher were saved. We rejoiced because this school now has three saved teachers and a Bible Club will soon form. One of the local churches will follow up on the new believers. We had another meeting tonight at the YMCA specifically for those with drug/alcohol problems. Three salvations and much ministry for deliverance etc. occurred. We drove back to Malcolm's home (about 2 hrs.) it was still snowing when we left Bratislava, but only rain in Partizanske. Fritz also has joined us. He will stay at Malcolm's and Friday morning after breakfast, we will leave for Austria for the weekend. We now have only one meeting left on Thursday in Slovakia.

Thursday, Apr. 4th-

The rain and snow has stopped, but it is still cold and cloudy. The sky cleared by mid-morning and the temperature warmed up to 50F by early afternoon. This is the warmest day since we've been here. After lunch we drove to the town of Prievizda (72,000) and passed out tracts and invitations to the meeting. Most of Malcolm's church people came and 7 people from the town came. It was a rather small meeting, but very fruitful for the Kingdom with six new salvations. And now the sadness of leaving our beloved Malcolm and Phyllis behind has filled our hearts. This is our last meeting in Slovakia.

Friday, Apr. 5th-

We had an early breakfast, and then we headed for Vienna Austria, stopping briefly in Bratislava along the way to see if we might find Monika. She's now been away from Fritz for five weeks. She stays with her brother in Bratislava or in Vienna when she gives piano lessons. If she's not in Bratislava we will continue on, have lunch in

Vienna and then another 3 ½ hours south of Vienna to Friesach where Fritz lives. We did not find Monika, so we had lunch in Bratislava, stopped at Vienna Airport to confirm our plane reservations, and headed south to Friesach. It was cloudy so we couldn't see most of the mountains. There was 30" of new snow in Klagenfurt where Fritz's work train is.(He is an engineer) We stopped there and he showed us his engines. It was 8:15 pm when we finally got to his house. He made us some very delicious Austrian pancakes for supper. I called home, and then a good night's sleep soon followed on a full belly. Diana came home at 8 am on the train. She works in western Austria. While she slept, Dave and I went into town, climbed a steep hill to a castle, and did some other hiking. Dave made the comment that "Ole Billy could not do this anymore as he was getting too old." (He is now 67 years old at the time of this trip. I am so very proud of him for his willingness and great stamina, to endure much travel, with little good rest and sleep. After lunch, we all went to a town where Diana works in the summer (resort hotel on a lake in the Austrian Alps). It was a sunny, warm afternoon. We spent the rest of the afternoon there; then we travelled back to Friesach for our last overnight stay with Fritz.

Saturday, Apr. 6th-

Dave and I had our last breakfast and prayer time with Fritz, before leaving for the train station. We spent some time playing stick hockey with some kids at the station before taking the 1 pm train to Vienna. What a wonderful time to rest and relax on this nice, smooth, quiet train to Vienna in our own private compartment. Dave's longtime friend Wolfgang met us at the Vienna train station. He brought us to his home, where we continued to rest and relax after our long, busy ministry time. We enjoyed a wonderful supper, a hot bath, and an early- to- bed night.

Sunday, Apr. 7th-

We awoke very refreshed and hungry. A nice Austrian breakfast was soon in our bellies. We went to church with Wolfgang and enjoyed just visiting but not speaking. We spent the rest of the day with he and his wife. An evening of prayer and precious fellowship followed. Dave was a bit saddened by now because he didn't think he would ever see his friend again. We went to bed early because we wanted to get a good night's sleep before travelling back to Boston the next day.

Monday, Apr. 8th-

We awoke and again were well-rested and refreshed. We got up early for breakfast because Wolfgang had to have us at the airport at 9 am for our flight back to the US.

We were very happy to head for home. The planes were right on time, and no problems. We landed in Boston at 4:10 pm and Clark drove us home, arriving at 8:30pm.

Chapter Five
1998

Sunday July 19, 1998

Another Missions trip has begun. This time, God has given me the great opportunity to visit Kenya, Africa for a whole month!!

Weeks and months of planning and preparations are now finished. I will travel with Jeremiah K., (A precious Brother and native Kenyan I met at the Annual Full Gospel Businessmen's Advance at Lake Morey, here in Vermont. We are leaving for Bradley Airport in Hartford, Connecticut at 12 noon from my home church: Renewed Life In Jesus.

Faith, myself and our children stopped in Brattleboro for lunch and then on to Bradley. Jeremiah K. showed up about 20 minutes before flight time and there was a big hurry to get his luggage checked in. By the time we did that, we had only 7 minutes left. There was hardly any time to say good-bye and we all but ran through security to get on the plane. It was a small commuter flight to JFK in New York City, and barely room to stand fully upright. And as we were taxiing out from the terminal, we saw three pieces of Jeremiah's luggage (the big box of Bibles, the keyboard and one huge suitcase) sitting on a cart on the tarmac. We told the flight attendant to please stop the plane but she threw her hands in the air and said, "I'm sorry, you'll have to make arrangements in New York." We had gotten there so late there was no time for them to load his bags. Plus they wouldn't check them all the way through to Nairobi. When we got to JFK we had to get the bags and report Jeremiah's missing stuff. They told us the bags would be sent to JFK on the next TWA flight in two hours. So we had to cancel our flight to London and book a late flight at 9:30 pm and wait for the luggage to come down from Bradley. It created a big hassle because JFK is so big we had to take a shuttle bus and taxi to the British Airways terminal twice from the TWA terminal. But all worked out ok. The flight to London was totally filled and we arrived at London's Heathrow Airport at about 9am London time.(**Monday July 20th**) It only took about six hours to get there. Jeremiah's friends were going to meet us at Heathrow at 7am, not knowing we had cancelled that flight. They had come to the airport and had breakfast prepared, but of course we missed everything. Jeremiah called them and they came and got us. We had a super time of fellowship and then we ate, took the subway into London and spent the whole afternoon sight-seeing. It's been thirty years since I was last in London, but all still looks the same. It was so good to ride on the very same tube (subway) line and see things I once saw before. Then we had a cheeseburger and fries at Burger King, went back to Jeremiah's friends flat, had more supper, and they took us back to Heathrow Airport. From there, we took a special coach bus (The famous Speed-Link) for a seventy minute ride across London to Gatwick Airport. That plane left around 10:30 pm London time and we flew all night to Nairobi Kenya arriving about 9:30 am Tuesday morning.

Tuesday, July 21st-Nairobi, Kenya Africa

Jeremiah's two sisters, another brother, and his father and about ten other people met us there. We spent all day in Nairobi because Jeremiah's brother had a doctor's appointment and we finally left for Jeremiah's at 5:30pm. We still hadn't slept since we left Vermont on Sunday. It took almost two hours to get to his house high in the hills, where the coffee and tea plantations flourish in the higher, cooler altitude. The roads are only like logging roads with washouts and huge pot holes. Most of the people walk. So far, I am the only white face I've seen.

The weather has been absolutely perfect, even in London - hot and sunny. We finally got to bed around 9:30pm Tuesday night which would be 1:30pm Vermont time. I slept nonstop for 13 hours

.Wednesday, July 22nd-

When I woke up it was sunny and warm. When I finally saw where we were (it was dark when we got here) it was so beautiful I could stay forever. It far exceeds the best of Florida. We are so far back in the hills. There is no electricity, no running water except one cold water faucet, no mail, no telephones except one or two in the area and they don't work very often. I'm the only white person here but all the people are so friendly. They go out of the way to greet me. We've been out walking and everybody wants to stop and talk. We've been through Jeremiah's dad's coffee and tea plantation. He will take us to where the coffee beans are sold to the coffee brokers and sent to the markets.

Thursday, July 23rd-

Our first 2 meetings were both church meetings - all believers, but with many prayer needs. The services are at 3pm because it gets dark by 6pm and they all use kerosene lanterns for light. The churches are dirt floors and just old cement or board buildings as the pictures will show. The worship services are very loud and boisterous, joy-filled, and much excitement. The preaching is very loud and lengthy.

Friday, July 24th-

Today is Friday already and I have a meeting today at 3pm. Jeremiah is in Nairobi making final arrangements for some larger meetings tomorrow and into the following weekend. So, I'm enjoying the warm sun and Jeremiah's sisters are cooking my breakfast while I write this. All travel for me is provided by a dear brother here named David. He comes to pick me up, translates for me, and brings me home. The food is delicious. Everything is grown right here and so fresh fruits, vegetables, chicken, beef, (no preservatives), no chemical sprays - you just wash everything first and its ok. I've not been sick, I feel absolutely well and strong, and am being well cared for. Praise the Lord for that. Last night I was invited to speak at a neighbor's funeral service. The whole village comes to the home and they have praise and worship, preaching, more praise and preaching until 2:30am. Since I'm the only white man most of these people have seen, they all want to know who I am and why I am here. I have been warmly received and loved and they are happy I came to share Jesus with them.

Saturday, July 25th-

Today we met with pastors and church leaders from over 100 churches. It was an all day teaching seminar dealing with church issues, ministry duties, etc. The meeting was very well received and the theme by the Holy Spirit seemed to focus on being a servant first, then lead. That was a very new concept to them and much weeping and repenting. In this culture, the man is absolute authority figure and all others serve him. But they were very willing to give it a try. They all seem to have a sweet teachable spirit.

Monday, July 27th-

I've been away from home a full week and I am really beginning to miss my family very much. If it were not for the Lord to help me, I could not do this.

We've had quite a lot of meetings over the weekend and we have another today and another tomorrow. Then we have a 3 day rest and then straight out for the next nine days after that.

I'm seeing the word of prophesy come to pass. This trip would be totally different than all the others. The difference this time is that all the meetings have been in local churches and I've been teaching and encouraging the believers. They are absolutely starving for the Word. It's the greatest need here. There are many good preachers and they get the people saved and excited, but no one to teach them.

After Tuesday's meeting, we'll have an opportunity to go to the higher mountains and forest where elephants and other animals live naturally. I've been here in the deep rural area for a week and still have not seen another white man. They all seem to go on safaris or stay in Nairobi. We are nearly 2 hours by car from Nairobi. Every night at 10:35pm, I here the British Airways flight to London. It leaves Nairobi at 10:25pm and 10 minutes later it passes directly overhead, still very low and climbing. That will be the flight I leave on, and I think about the joy of coming home every night it flies over us. However, the Lord still has much more for us to do for now.

Tuesday July 28th-

Today is our last meeting (officially) until Sunday. Jeremiah and I have been speaking together and taking turns who will speak first. Today Jeremiah spoke first, but stopped after only 5 minutes. He suddenly gave me the pulpit and I preached about Jairus's daughter and the woman with the issue of blood. At the end, people ran to the front for prayer; many who had been sick, 4 wanted baptism of Holy Spirit, and one lady who was totally deaf in one ear had her hearing totally restored. Many in that church have known for years she was deaf and they were so excited for her. Then, after the meeting, as we were walking from the church, a young woman came along and she wanted to be saved, so that was a full evening of ministry.

Wednesday, July 29th -

Today we have a rest day -wash clothes, read, drink Kenya tea, hang around - relax.

Thursday, July 30th -

Today is very special day for me. It is our 21st wedding anniversary. This is the first one that I have been away from my Sweetie and my heart yearns to be with her. God will give us both grace and comfort in the Holy Spirit to help us until we can be together again on August 12th. We took Jeremiah's father's car into Nairobi for repairs because we hit a very deep hole and tore off the muffler and tailpipe. We left the car at a local garage and spent the rest of the morning making connections and speaking arrangements for the crusade/convention next week which will begin Tuesday and end Sunday night, August 9th. People will stay all night and there will be 4 meetings each day.

It took until Friday 5:30pm before it was ready. So we spent 2 days in the city. It is a very large city - 1 million 700 thousand people. I saw lepers, beggars, people sleeping on the sidewalks, people picking through garbage heaps for scraps of food, people with no place to live. Unemployment is high - nearly 40%. People come to the city in hope of work and many don't find any. Street crime such as robbery, pickpockets etc, is very high, and when they see an American, he is a prime target. But God has cared for me and protected me from all harm, just as His Word says in Psalm 91.

Friday, July 31st-

We continued making arrangements for other crusades in the coming months. We rode around in the city in small van/bus type vehicle called a Mattatu. It was very crowded but cheap. We also walked a lot and I got to see much of Nairobi several times. Later, when we got the car back, we drove 1 hour north to spend the night with Esther's sister and father. It was quite cold there so I'm glad I brought some warm clothes with me.

Saturday, Aug. 1st-

Today we drove to the Rift Valley. It is a huge are of plains surrounded by volcano peaks. We drove to an overlook place 8,000 feet high. It was very hazy and clouds were over the tops of the mountains, but I still took some pictures. Then we came back home to Jeremiah's father's house. I hadn't slept very well the other 2 nights and it was good to re-visit the bed I've been sleeping in.

Sunday, Aug. 2nd-

This morning, a local pastor (one who has been translating for me) took me to preach the morning service and then I went to his house for the rest of the day and overnight and he brought me back this Monday morning.

Monday, Aug. 3rd-

I'm getting excited now because meetings begin tomorrow and I'll be going home next Tuesday. I can hardly wait to see my family at the airport.

God has given me such a wonderful family of believers here too. Everywhere around me, there are so many Christians, sometimes whole villages. What a difference that would make in America.

This afternoon, we will be finalizing the speaking arrangements and more prayer. It's been cold 50 degrees and raw wind/ rain since Saturday, so I'm glad the meetings have moved inside.

Tuesday, Aug. 4th-

It is cool, cloudy, and rainy this morning. Jeremiah and I did the second session - only 35 to 40 people attended because most are working. Then we went to Nairobi again to cash some traveler's checks and went to see a backslidden sister at a restaurant. We've been encouraging her to repent and come back to the Lord and He is stirring her heart. I'll try to go on Monday one last time.

Wednesday-Thursday, Aug. 5th and 6th-

Both meetings on both days we spoke early - 9am to 11am. There were more people this time and we also fellowshipped with some brethren from Nairobi. This afternoon, there is some sadness in Jeremiah's house. His sister Margaret is flying back to America tonight from Nairobi at 10:15pm on KLM to Amsterdam (all night flight) and will have an 8 hour layover then on to Boston. She lives in Rhode Island where she goes to college and works. She has been there for 3 years and she came home for 30 days. So her family was sad to see her leave again. When the flight left, we heard it pass directly over this house, followed soon after the flight we'll be taking. Jeremiah and his father, brother, and his other sister Naomi took Margaret to the airport and stayed the night in Nairobi.

Friday, Aug. 7th-

This morning is cool, but the clouds are breaking. I'll be speaking at the 4-6pm session tonight and that will be the last meeting for me; unless I'm asked to speak at a church Sunday morning. I am getting really anxious to come home now that all the meetings are finished, but I can still enjoy the few days I have left here. We got to the meeting a little late because the roads are so bad, but it was a very fruitful meeting - many souls were saved and others prayed for. Many wanted prayer for sickness and power to live a Christian life. I spent Saturday with Peter (at the house).

Sunday, Aug. 8th-

Well, I thought there would be no more meetings for me to speak at, but at the last moment last night, I was asked to do the morning service at the big Anglican Church where Jeremiah's dad attends. It's the mother church over 5 others in the surrounding area. The text of my message was all from Colossians Chapter 3:1-17. This turned out to be a very fitting "closing" meeting with nearly 400 in attendance. They did not however, allow me the opportunity to pray for anyone since they do not do that in their church.

Monday, Aug. 9th-

Jeremiah, Naomi, and I went into Nairobi so Jeremiah could take Peter to see his doctor. We spent all day in town, bought lunch and found some good ice cream. That night I was invited to attend a 35 year wedding anniversary party. We stayed until nearly midnight, so I didn't get a long night's sleep before Tuesday's all night flight to London.

Tuesday, Aug. 10th-

The big day has finally arrived and I can hardly wait. I have everything packed. Naomi would not allow me to carry anything to the car. She absolutely insisted on carrying everything for me. Many photographs were taken and we left for Nairobi at about 2:30pm. Jeremiah wanted to meet with Esther's sister for last minute shopping.

We got to the airport at 7:30pm. There were armed soldiers on the access road and inside the terminal. (Extra security since the U.S. Embassy in Nairobi and Tanzinia was blown up a few days back). My luggage was opened and searched and all was cleared through. The extra security made the flight late, but I was onboard and left at 11:10pm. Jeremiah remained behind for further ministry there in Nairobi. My flight back to London and the connecting flight to JFK went perfectly all the way. I took the commuter shuttle back to Hartford, CT and arrived 10 minutes early. Faith and the kids met me at the airport. We took one of Jeremiah's suitcases back to Esther's and drove north toward home, stopping for Pizza in Bellows Falls. We got home about 7pm.

Chapter Six
2001

Wednesday, Mar. 7th, 2001 –

My first trip to India begins -

John Coppola picked me up at home at 9:20am and we drove to Kennedy airport in N.Y.C. We made very good time until we got to out skirts of N.Y.O. at about 2:15pm. Then a massive traffic jam which lasted until nearly 6pm. We almost ran out of gas waiting in traffic and I got to the airport at 6:40pm. My flight was to leave at 7:30pm so it was very close, but I got on board in time. I had a good flight across the Atlantic, arriving in Frankfurt, Germany where I am now, waiting my 2 hours before continuing on to Bombay, India. It's now **Thur. March 8th, 10am Germany time** (4am Vermont time). It's cloudy and cool about 45 degrees. No snow here but I did see some before we landed. They're cleaning up the same plane and putting on meals for the flight.

Our flight to Bombay leaves at exactly 11:30am for the 7 hour and 15 minute trip to Bombay. It was very beautiful because it was day time and very few clouds. Our trip took us across Eastern Europe, then slightly southeast across the Black Sea in Russia. It is a huge body of water and took us a very long time to cross it even at 570mph. Then we turned south and traveled over the entire length of Iran on toward the western coast of India, arriving in Bombay just about 11:55pm India time. This is a very different climate with warmth and humidity, even at midnight. But it feels so good to be where it's warm. I had to take a bus from the international terminal to the domestic terminal having to pass through customs and immigration because Bombay was the port of entry. I had about 1 ½ hours to wait for the flight to Bangalore which left Bombay on **Friday Mar. 9th at 3:15am,** arriving in Bangalore at 5:30am. Sharad, his wife Prema, and two of his older daughters were there to greet me at the airport. They put long strings of flowers around my neck as an India custom to welcome visitors to their country. Then we went to their house for tea and breakfast and fellowship. Sharad's family then asked if I would share from the Word of God with all of them before his 3 younger girls went to school. I still hadn't slept since I left Vermont on Wednesday and now it is Friday morning. He took me into the city to pick up the posters and flyers for the seminars. We traveled in a rickshaw but these things are like a 3-wheel motor bike with a passenger carriage. It was the ride of my life. They drive very fast, everybody cuts in and out, passing buses, trucks, cars, bicycles, motor bikes, people walking, cows lying down right in the road, no stop lights or stop signs at intersections. They drive on the left side of the road here. We had a really great time getting to know each other, fellowshipping. I took a little 2 hour nap in the afternoon. Their oldest daughter Grace gave me her bed and she slept on the concrete floor on a straw mat in the livingroom. What a loving and wonderful host family they are to me. Until **Saturday afternoon Mar. 10th**, we just visited and fellowshipped. Pastor Sharad, Prema, and I went into the city (Bangalore) to buy water and food for the 14 days we will spend in Talavadi. Mid-afternoon, we hired a driver and 4 wheel drive vehicle to take Sharad, his wife and myself to the remote village of Talavadi, 220 miles southeast of Bangalore. The journey was a very long, bumpy, 7 ½ hour ride, before we finally arrived around 10pm. This house is where his Bible school is and where we will stay. From here, we also go out into the surrounding jungle villages for meetings.

Sunday, Mar. 11th-

We had our church meeting and then in the afternoon, we hired a driver and Jeep to take us to a gypsy colony about 20 miles from here. The roads are very rough and mostly washed out and it took about an hour to get there. We met under a thatched roof hut and close to 35 gypsies crowded in to hear the Word. We praised together also, and then laid hands on each person, including all of those who were sick. Many received immediate healing including one old woman who was paralyzed on the whole right side of her body. From there, we went to another village 10 more miles away and had a home meeting with about 30 people jammed in like sardines. What a wonderful time of Praise, sharing and praying for their sick, followed with a long ride home after 8:30pm on the dark way back through the jungle forest. We stayed up talking until 11:30pm.

Monday, Mar. 12th-

Another warm, still morning and I begin teaching all day in the Bible school. We'll still go out to another remote village every night. It's very hot here. On Sunday, it was about 105 degrees Fahrenheit.

We are very far inland away from Bangalore so there's almost no breeze to stir the air in the forest jungle. I have a ceiling fan so even though it's hot, the night gets cool for sleeping. The house is like where I stayed in Kenya. No running water and an inside squat hole for toilet. Since I lived in Africa, I quickly made myself right at home. My bed is a steel slab with a one inch thick pad. The bed is up off the floor, because of rats and snakes which come in at night. But the Blood of Jesus keeps me safe. I sleep very well and look forward to each new day the Lord gives me. I wake up very early every morning to pray. Also at 5am, there is a call to prayer for the Muslims. The have a high tower with a loud-speaker and a man speaks and chants for nearly 15 minutes. This town of Talavadi is 80% Hindu, 19% Muslim and 1% Christian. Today (Monday) I taught from 9am to 4:30pm in the Bible school class. We are teaching on "the anointing" "spiritual gifts", and then "motivational gifts". The day went extremely well. Every student wanted to receive the baptism of the Holy Spirit. So we prayed and asked God to impart the gift. They all received.

Tuesday, Mar. 13th-

It's 7:15am. A strange thing happened today. I awoke at 3:00am and was very awake and alert. I began to pray and during that time, I began to cry for a long time. Then at 5am, the loud-speaker began. But it was different, and all the dogs began to howl, children began to cry and act up, a general restlessness seemed to settle in. I continued to pray and observe the occurrences. Then I saw a vision. Men were coming toward our house and they got very close, they reached forth their hands to touch the outside walls and suddenly pulled their hands back as though they felt something hot like our stove. No matter how many times they tried to touch the house, they could not. Then the vision vanished. When Sharad and Prema got up, they told me today and for the next 2 days it is a Hindu festival. At 3am, their priests walk to the 4 sides of the village in only a loin cloth, covering themselves with ashes. They take the blood of a goat and mix it with cooked rice and throw it into the air as they walk. They do this to release demonic spirits upon the people and prepare them for the festival. They have blocked off the streets so no car or Bus can pass through and then they set up places for walking through fire and hot coals. Until I was told, I knew nothing about this. But the Lord woke me up at the exact moment the priests were loosing the spirits. We all

3 had a fervent time of prayer for covering and including all the Bible students. Today our first teaching is on discerning of spirits. Today went very well. The students had already a good foundation and are learning very quickly. When they come into the classroom, the come a half hour early and sit quietly and pray. How wonderful that would be to see our church like this. We went to a Hindu village tonight and to two home cell groups. We saw a woman there that I had prayed for Sunday in church. She had a huge growth on her throat and could not speak. But when we saw her tonight, the growth was completely gone and she was speaking normally. Even Sharad was amazed. But we serve a wonderful all mighty God. There are many demon spirits in Hindu people and so its so common that they want to be freed. Jesus sets them free very quickly. I've already experienced this several times and again tonight. On our way back to our house, there were many ox-carts going along with loads of wood. Tomorrow they will make a huge pile and start the fire to their goddess. There is much screaming and drum beating tonight.

Wednesday, Mar. 14th-

It's 7:30am and I'm up and ready for our next teaching session. I think we will finish the "spiritual gifts" today. The students are coming in now. We have a good time of praise and worship for 45-50 minutes then we begin the class work. I had another wonderful day with the students. We finished "spiritual gifts" and began the "motivational gifts" teaching. Sharad, Prema, myself, and 4 of the brothers including my interpreter went to two cell home group meetings tonight. We have to hire a vehicle each time because these villages are quite far away and very remote. I saw the first wild animal tonight. It was only a monkey, but kinda neat to see it. Also, one of the villages only has 19 houses and is totally Hindu. Not one Christian. But we were welcomed to come and share the Word with them and pray for their sick. I have never seen so many people healed so quickly on any trip before this one. These cell group meetings are the beginnings of 6 new church plantings, and 2 more by next week. Sharad has totally and willingly asked me to receive all these new churches under our spiritual covering and authority, so within the next 2 years Renewed Life will be the spiritual father of 8 new churches in India, providing most of the materials taught in the Bible school also. What an honor and privilege!! I believe I'll be coming back here more often to oversee the work as it continues. They want very much for me to do this. When we go back to Bangalore, the first 6 churches will be officially registered with the Indian government.

Thursday, Mar. 15th-

I am having another wonderful day with the students. We are all becoming very close together in the Lord. We finished "motivational gifts" and then one study in the afternoon on "words". Tonight we went out again to rural village to share the Word and heal the sick. When they know we are coming, they go through their village and bring their sick for healing. 2 times, because of God's miracle working power, I've been asked to pray and anoint bottles of oil to leave behind when I leave so they can anoint the sick with it. They believe their sick will be healed because of this. Just like the account of Paul anointing the handkerchief in book of Acts. I've met and prayed for several village leaders and very blessed by their wisdom and hospitality. It's so difficult to even write about all I've seen here, but, never since I've been a Christian, have I ever seen the like of this!!

Friday, Mar. 16th-

It's 6:45am and I've been up since 5:30 today. I've been restudying teaching on Colossians 1-5 to teach the class. We have only four days of school until they graduate next Wednesday. They are all new believers and I have the honor of water-baptizing them all this Sunday. We'll have an all day outside service beginning with gathering of all six churches for praise, worship, Word, prayer, communion, then the baptisms then all afternoon eating and fellowship. We will all meet at the local river by the big dam for this day.

Tonight, we will visit 2 more remote villages for praise, Word, and prayer. All of these evening meetings are so special. We gather at one house, outside on the concrete slab like a porch. They lay down straw mats to sit on. I'm learning how to do this without my knee joints popping out. When the people up in these small rural villages know we are coming, they come from their homes and gather their sick to be prayed for, just like the people used to do when Jesus came to a village. Many of these sick people are healed immediately. It is such a joy to be where people will sit for hours waiting for us to come and bring them the Presence of God. Their hunger and thirst for Him is like nothing I have ever seen in America since I've been saved for 18 years. They have such strong faith to believe God will really come with us, and He will provide all of their needs.

Saturday, Mar. 17th -

9am- No Bible School classes today, so we have a free day. Sharad, Prema and I went to a place with a phone early this morning. We called his family in Bangalore. Grace will send home an email for me. Also, Sharad's married daughter, Joy, will come here by bus with her husband Dominic. We expect them around 2-3pm. They left Bangalore at 5am and it's about 9 hours with 3 bus changes. When they arrive, we will ordain and anoint the leaders of the 6 new churches. So we won't have any outside meetings tonight.

Something else I learned today about the culture here. Every morning and evening, I have noticed that the women brush away everything with a small broom of dried palm fronds from in front of the door to the house. Since there is only a single dirt road between each row of houses, this is difficult to do. There are oxen/carts, cows, goats, chickens all going by all the time, so there is much dung to sweep away. Then the women mix cow dung and water and sprinkle/wet the area in front of the door. They do this because they believe it will keep away evil spirits because cows are considered holy/sacred. Then they take white pigment and mark in front of the door to let the evil spirits know that that cannot enter the home. (Thank God for the Blood of Jesus).

Sunday, Mar. 18th -

5am- I woke up early for prayer/Word. We had breakfast at 7:30 and all 10 Bible students and 12 others want to be baptized so we hired a large Jeep to take us to the dam for baptism. We transported 12 on the first trip and 10 on the next trip. And some from the church took the bus. It was absolutely beautiful there as the pictures will show. The water was warm and the presence of The Lord was mighty. We then had the regular Sunday service with communion, and then lunch. At 4:30 we leave to go to another remote village to preach and heal the sick.

This meeting was very powerful. The Spirit of God manifested upon all of us with great refreshing and strength. Much praise, worship, then the Word, and then we prayed for the sick. We were much encouraged by their testimonies from when we were there last Sunday night. Many received instant healing, so tonight, they brought 6 more sick people to pray for them. I know the Lord healed them also. Never on any other trip have I seen so many miraculous healings, place to place, one after the other.

Monday, Mar. 19th -

Up early to pray and study before class. Also, Joy and Dominic are leaving on early bus at 6am, so I want to be up to say good-bye. They have 3 day train journey to northern India to preach and teach. They will not be back again before I leave on the 29th from Bangalore. I'll be staying here all this week in Talavadi. School finishes this Wednesday at noon. Graduation of the students will be on Thursday, then outside crusade/seminars on Friday and Saturday.

Tonight we'll be going out to a village we haven't visited yet. What a super meeting. I preached about Nicodemus and John 3 and nine people got saved plus many sick prayed for.

Tuesday, Mar. 20th -

6am - Time to pray and study. Today we'll be teaching from Ted Davis' "What I am and have in Christ Jesus." Later today, the rest of Sharad's family will come here. They will be coming for the graduation ceremony. We probably won't be going out tonight, but I don't know that for sure.

Wednesday, Mar. 21st -

6am - We had 2 house meetings last night and prayed for the sick. Sharad's family did not come yesterday - they will come late today. It's 9 to 9 ½ hours by bus from Bangalore. Today, we'll review in school. We'll be finished by noon. Later this afternoon, there will be a graduation rehearsal. Tonight we will have another house meeting and then no more. Some free time Thursday and then the graduation. Friday and Saturday will be all day seminars. So far, nearly 200 people have returned their registration forms, so it looks like a good turnout. We'll be putting up a tent-like tarp called a pandal so the meetings can be held outside. It's hot now everyday; (105F to 107F). It's soon to be the rainy season, but so far, only a few sprinkles one day more than a week ago. We heard there was an elephant which came in from the forest. Poachers had tried to rip off its tusks, and he got away. We didn't see him, but other villagers saw him. It seems like now my time here is running out quickly. I'll be going back to Bangalore on Sunday after church. Then free day on Monday, Tuesday and Wednesday and we'll have our seminars there. Close to 1,500 people expected for those. And then I fly out at 8:30pm on Thursday.

Thursday, Mar. 22nd -

6:15 am – It's very still and warm outside. We had our last house meeting last night. About 30 people received the baptism in the Holy Spirit. Then I was taken to 2 other houses close by to pray for their sick. I know for sure the Lord has healed them. Everyday, we've gotten word that the Lord healed all the sick we prayed for from the previous night. The men came in the night to set up the pandal. It's quite big, like a tent, and filled with plastic chairs. The graduation program is from 11-1, and then we will all have lunch together. Then all the visitors go back to their villages by buses. The program went wonderfully. But before it started, a man came to the house in very deep depression and suicidal, but the Lord was so gracious and merciful to him. He received Jesus and the Lord then filled him with much joy and a new hope. The man then stayed for the graduation service. We were expecting about 125 - 150 people, but more than 250 came. We didn't have enough chairs, and some of the food ran a little short, but at least everyone did get something to eat. And then it happened: I was sitting inside the house, and people came inside for prayer for all kinds of sickness and body pains etc. One after another they came, until well after 3:30. Word has gotten out about all the healings and even sick Hindus are coming to be healed. I have never seen anything like this since I've been saved. It's drawn so much attention that a news reporter with a video camera came and video-taped a lot of the people as they were being prayed for. Then he himself asked for prayer for his work and business. Two other villages have sent for us to come to pray for their sick, so tonight, we will be going out again. Then the 2 day seminar starts tomorrow. (See Matthew 4:23-24)

Friday, Mar. 23rd -

6:15am - The 2 house meetings were awesome. I shared from Matthew 6:24-34 and then prayed for the sick and we went to the second house, just across the road from the first. They had brought other sick people and were waiting for us to come. Before we finished there, a man from the first house came running over. We had prayed for him for severe back pain, he was slightly bowed over and could not sit or move without much pain. But God totally healed him and he came running to tell us. So he had a great testimony for the others as we continued to pray for them.

Today, we have the seminars. We'll start at 10am and break for lunch at 12:30-2. Then there will be 1 more session until 4pm followed by a time of prayer for the people. We have provided lunch for all because many have come by bus from the remote villages where we have been going out at night for the house meetings, so I recognize many of the people. We've been twice at least to their houses in the last 2 weeks. I hope there will be enough room for everyone. If they don't all fit under the tent it's frying hot in the sun. Everyday now it's above 100 degrees. Summer has begun and we are very far inland and south of Bangalore. Last night there were some thunderstorms in the mountains to the east of us. Much lightening and some rumblings of thunder but, no rain here yet.

Saturday, Mar. 24th -

6:30am – It is another very warm/humid morning. Yesterday's seminar was awesome. About 150 people had returned the registration forms, but 235 people showed up. They too, came by bus, some from as far as 30 miles away. There were so many people, and it took a long time for lunch so we only had one session in the afternoon. I taught about blind Bartimeaus and the Spirit of God moved in like the wind and a cloud. 9 people got saved, at least 180-200 got baptized in the Holy Spirit, and then Barnabas and I began praying for the sick. Over 200 people wanted prayer so we had to make two lines. I started praying one on one at 2:40 and non-stop until the last was prayed for at 4:30. Some of the people missed their buses and had to stay overnight with relatives. The man with the video camera will be back again and the photographer. These meeting will be spoken of in local papers, and the people keep telling others of the miracles and healings, so it keeps multiplying. No telling how many will come today.

Sunday, Mar. 25th-

4:05am - I've been awake since 2:45 am. My head is so full of what I've seen and experienced of the presence of God, that I just can't go back to sleep. Yesterday's meeting was absolutely of biblical proportion. I have never since I've been saved seen such throngs of people so desperately hungry for the touch of God on their lives. People began arriving by bus from the other rural villages about 9:30am. Some from the gypsy colony came first. They live in thatched roof shacks. I've been twice to their camp. Word has spread about the miracles of God and people began to pile in. There were many more than 320 in the tent (only 150 chairs) many couldn't get in, so they were just outside. We waited until 10:30 before starting and then served them all tea for refreshment. At 10:45 we started with praise and worship. Then, so many people who had got healed the day before, or in their homes where I was taken to pray for them, wanted to give testimony. One in particular - a man who had lain crippled on a mat for two years. He was totally miraculously healed and came nearly 35 miles on a bus to testify. But when he stood up to talk, he was so overcome with joy that all he could do was cry. We have many photos taken by the reporter including this very man. When testimonies were finished, I did "The Sower and the Seed" parable. After this teaching, Barnabas and I invited those who wanted prayer to come forward. The crowd came suddenly toward us and jammed us against the wall, there were so many. We prayed for each one individually and it took nearly two and a half hours before we were finished. The photos will show much more than I can describe in this little book. I prayed for just about everything one could imagine-from all manner of sickness and disease, aids, young boy in a coma (whom God raised up on the spot), runaway husbands, drunkenness, drugs, wives beaten, abused, and raped, salvations, baptism in the Holy Spirit, demon possession and oppression, lameness, blind, deaf, mute, retarded, and the list goes on. In nearly every case, the Lord healed them right then. Some brought bottles of oil or water. They wanted me to anoint the bottles with God's Presence so they could use the contents for healing after I'm gone. Never ever before have I seen Jesus'days so alive in my life. After this, I think I'll not ever be the same again. I don't even know now how I'll go back home and pastor such a quiet little church where we can hardly get eight people to show up for a Wednesday night Bible Study!! (Just my thoughts right now as I write this).

There were no less than 30-40 people jammed and crowded together sitting cross-legged on the floor at every house meeting-two per night, six days a week for two weeks, including the sick the villagers had brought for healing. It's no small wonder why miracles happen here. I'm thinking now about the people who stood in 105F for up to two hours before I ever got to pray for the last one in the line. In our home church, some cannot wait for the door to open as soon as it's prayer time for the sick. I ask myself "What's wrong with this picture?" Now I understand what happened to my friend Joanne after her trip to Haiti.

Today I'll be presenting the message for the Sunday service, and then we'll head back to Bangalore. I'd really like to stay here for the rest of my time, but seminars have been arranged in the city, so I can't stay here. I won't be surprised to see 250 people at least show up for church. The men came last night and took the tent down, so if these people all come to church and then want prayer, I think it will be a very long day, plus the 7 hour drive back to Bangalore.

(Later)-We had a wonderful church service today; only just the regular members came so it was small and nice. I talked about "Holding Fast the Profession of Our Faith" and we all held onto a long piece of rope to illustrate the point of the message. Many tears and crying because we all knew this was the last time we'd all be together. Then one of the new believers wanted to be water baptized, so we took him to the river and I went in with him and baptized him. We came back to the house, finished packing, loaded up, prayed, and left for Bangalore at about 12:45pm. We stopped in two different villages to pray for the sick in two houses. We also stopped along the highway for a picnic lunch, arriving in Bangalore at 8:45pm. Fifteen minutes after our arrival, the electric went off so I couldn't send/receive any e-mails.

Monday, Mar. 26th-

6am-It's very warm here in the city. Hazy and smelly pollution from all the traffic has soon clogged my nose and throat. We went out early and I sent an e-mail home. We also tried to make arrangements for the seminar but nothing came together, so we have arranged some house meetings instead. We all went shopping later and got back about 7pm. We were all tired and went to bed early.

Tuesday, Mar. 27th-

6am-Warm again this morning. I plan to send another e-mail home today; also reconfirm flight reservations for Thursday night. Sharad and I are going into the city later. He wants to buy a new guitar for the ministry. We are also going to have a house meeting tonight at 6:30pm.

Wednesday, Mar. 28th-

6:15am-Very hot and sticky. The power went out at 7:30am and never came back on until sometime in the night, so none of the ceiling fans worked. We did, however, have a very good meeting. Nearly forty people came and most of them wanted prayer for sickness or for other things. The Lord was very powerful in His Presence among us. Today is my last full day and night here. We don't have any other plans that I am aware of. My flights were confirmed yesterday. More people from the neighborhood wanted me to come and pray for them. Then we all went out to a Chinese restaurant for an awesome supper. There were twelve of us in all!!

Thursday, Mar. 29th-

6:15am- My last day here. Everyone in the house is sad and teary-eyed. It seemed like all we did was watch the clock. I did go into the city to a Christian book and music store. I got some good praise cassettes for about $1.25 each. Then we had lunch about 1:30pm. All Sharad's family gift-wrapped the things they bought for my family. We also celebrated Hannah's birthday three days early so I could be here for it. I finished packing and what a load! Each of my suitcases is filled to the max. We left Sharad's flat at 5:30pm for the airport and all ten of us waited together until it was time for me to pass through the final security checkpoint. It was very emotionally difficult to leave. After spending three weeks with this precious family, we all got pretty attached to each other. The plane left right on time and I arrived in Bombay at 10:05 pm. Then I had a long wait. But Customs/Immigration took nearly two hours, plus having to recheck my luggage. The flight to Frankfurt Germany also left right on time, arriving early Friday morning.

Friday, Mar. 30th-

It's 8:30am Germany time (4½ hours behind India time). I'm sitting in the boarding gate area and will depart in about 1½ hours from now, arriving at JFK 12:15pm US time. At 40 degrees F, it feels very cold here because that's about 60 degrees colder than where I just came from. I'll have six more time zones to fly west through. I did get some sleep on the ten hour flight from India so I don't feel too tired yet, and I can sleep some more across the Atlantic Ocean. It's now 9am here (3am New York). The Boarding Gate is now open so it's time to move on. It was a wonderful flight across the ocean, crossing over southwestern Scotland, northern Ireland, and on toward the southern tip of Greenland . I could clearly see all the polar ice cap and the breaking up of the ice pack into huge icebergs far below us (38,000 feet). Then we flew on over Labrador and turned south across northeastern Canada, into Maine; and then along the coast toward the eastern end of Long Island. It got cloudy the rest of the way to JFK and the clouds extended down to 760 feet above the land/water below us. One could see nothing more from looking out the windows. Once we descended below the clouds, we were just above the waters of Jamaica Bay and could see big waves and whitecaps, so I could tell it was windy and stormy. When we landed, it was 36F and a wind-driven rain. But at least I was nearly home by now. After getting my luggage, it was on to Customs/Immigration. I was soon out of this area and John C. was waiting for me and we soon began our trip to Vermont. It was a cold, windy rain until we reached central Mass. and it turned to freezing rain, then snow. It took us seven hours to drive home from JFK and ten inches of new wet, heavy snow—welcome home Rick. I had hoped it would have been all gone by now. But all in all, it was another wonderful trip and I experienced much in the Presence of the Lord.

Chapter Seven
2002

Friday, Sept. 6th, 2002 –

This year's trip to India has begun. After a 4 hour ride to Logan with Faith and Skinners, I was quickly processed through to my gate area. It's now 4:35pm and my flight boards at 6:30pm, so now the waiting begins. This flight takes me to London, then change for the flight to Bombay. **7:45am – (Sat. London time**). After a smooth flight, I am here at Heathrow. It's raining and the temperature is 57 degrees. I'm waiting now for the 10:40am departure to Bombay. A very timely flight brought me safely into Bombay at **12:05am (Sun. India time).** It is warm and humid with very light rain sprinkles. After going through customs and riding on the shuttle bus to the Domestic Terminal, I had only 30 minutes to catch my flight to Bangalore, arriving at 4:30am. Pastor Sharad and all his family greeted me there and we came back to his house for breakfast and fellowship. Then at 8am, I went to bed for 4 hours of much needed sleep. We visited and ate supper and fellowshipped more until 10pm and all of us were ready for bed.

Monday, Sept. 9th -

A warm and partly cloudy morning awaits us. After breakfast, Sharad and I went into the city to cash my traveler's checks. Now we are loading the hired vehicle to take us to Talavadi. A long 7 hour trip awaits us. And then tomorrow I will begin to teach the Bible class "Fail Proof Living".

After a long drive, we arrived tonight in Talavadi. It was wonderful to greet the 4 pastors I ordained last year and to meet the students tonight. It feels very good to finally be here after leaving Chester last Friday at noon.

Tuesday, Sept. 10th -

5:15am - As last year, the Muslims begin their day with the call to prayer from the loud speakers, so there's no chance of sleeping later. So it's up to pray, study and prepare for the teaching in the classroom. We had a very good day, but today I was told some not so good news. Since I was here last year, the Muslims want to kill me. 5 Arab men came to this village only 5 weeks ago and began to speak over loud speakers to watch for any American and kill him. The local Muslims remembered I was here last year. The local people called me "Father Abraham" and my name was given to be watched for. Sharad has put me in a room in the very back of the house instead of in the front room I had last year. I cannot go outside of the house in the daytime. They have 4 watchmen here now while I'm here. 2 sleep while the others are awake. They are here to protect me and take me out the back of the house if Muslims come here. They took me under cover of darkness to a rural village last night, and this will be the plan. They tell no one else when I'm coming. We will not be having any outside meetings including the student's graduation. They have cancelled the plans to distribute all the posters for meetings with my picture on them. We will have the graduation inside and only a few people will receive notice. As soon as I finish teaching Fail Proof Living, the students will be told graduation will be the next day. There is much prayer for last month for God's protection for me. So looks like we will finish on Thursday and have the graduation on Friday early morning, and then Sharad, Prema, and I will be taken back to Bangalore. I'll still visit small villages at night until I leave to see the people who came to our meetings last year. It's a very strange feeling to be here, knowing Muslims are looking to see me without these 4 men. I'm not afraid at all and this is really a miracle in itself. I have great peace and plan to finish all the ministry before we leave on Friday. The people in the village where we went to last night were all Hindu and they loved and welcomed us with joy into their home. The Muslims won't go there because they are greatly outnumbered. But since last year, this village of Talavadi has been taken over by Muslims. So right now, it looks like I cannot come back here. (Present observation-subject to change) Sharad and his family are also being watched and have become a possible target because of the Bible School and because I am staying with them. There was a great uproar among the Muslims after I left last year because of all the miracles God did for the Hindu people. They are still stirred up about it. So today, I'll continue teaching, and after dark, I'll go to another village to someone's home to speak and to pray for the sick. Last night's meeting was very special because the family who invited me had attended last year's outside meetings. The woman could not speak and last year, God totally healed her and she has spoken perfectly ever since. There is a photo of me on a shelf in her living room. Also, last night, there was one sick woman, 2 sick children. Jesus also broke a Hindu curse off that whole family and I anointed every doorway in the house with oil and we plead the blood of Jesus to keep out all evil spirits.

Wednesday, Sept. 11th-

Tonight after dark, I was taken to a home in another village. I had been there twice when I was here last time. It was so good to see these people again. This was one of the cell groups which has recently become a church. As Sharad and Barnabas played their guitars and we all worshiped, the Holy Spirit came gently upon us and He touched and ministered to the people. There was much prayer for broken, hurting families and sickness, and prayers to bless all the children.

Thursday, Sept. 12th -

Today I will continue the “Fail Proof Living” teaching. The students have been going to the home meetings also so they have the opportunity to see how God has met the needs of the people. I think tonight, we will visit the gypsy camp. Last year, one of them got saved and we baptized her. They received me very lovingly last year, came to all our outside meetings, so I’m looking forward to seeing them again.

At 5:30pm we went to a tiny Hindu low-caste village instead. It was 45 minutes away through the deep forest. We were there last year also. This is another of the churches that have been started. We prayed for several sick people, and blessed and prayed for all the children. Also saw the young boy (last year was crippled and could not walk) now he is very well - he runs and plays with all the other kids.

Friday, Sept. 13th -

5:15am - Muslim speakers wake us all for the day. Today we will finish “Fail Proof Living” and my teaching is the last to do before students graduate on Monday. All of Sharad’s kids have Monday off from school, so they will come here for the graduation, then we’ll all ride back to Bangalore together. Tonight we went to the gypsy camp. It’s quite far from here and took about an hour with our hired bus. Last year there I had prayed for a young girl who could not walk or speak, and now she is perfectly well. Also an older woman who could not speak but now she can. Tonight, close to 50 gypsies came with many needs for healing. It was a very crowded small room. I'll be expecting to hear some good reports by Sunday because some of them will be coming to church. It was 9:15pm when we got back and a late supper. So it's bedtime now at 10:20pm.

Saturday, Sept. 15th -

6:15am - Got to sleep a little longer today because school is finished. Quiet day, then we'll be going to another village tonight.

Sunday, Sept. 16th -

5:15am - Another good house meeting last night. Many prayed for-sickness, family problems, and for couple to have a baby.

Today, early, we'll be going to the dam to baptize 6 new believers then we'll have the regular church meeting when we return. Some of the new believers from the gypsy camp to be baptized did not come, so after waiting for them, we had church first and then took 3 to baptize. Then we came back, dedicated George's second child and had communion. Tonight we had another meeting in a village and prayed for the sick. Sharad's family was to leave Bangalore at 5am Monday to come here for the student's graduation on Tuesday morning and then we would all leave together to go back to Bangalore. But tonight we heard about transportation strike in Bangalore. No buses, trains, or taxis, and all businesses shut down, so they cannot come and we cannot get back to Bangalore because we need to hire our transportation. I don't know how long the strike will last, but my flight doesn't leave until Thursday night so there's still some time left.

Monday, Sept. 17th -

5:30am - Good news has come. Sometime during the night, the police arrested the man who organized the strike, so Sharad's family left Bangalore about 2am and should be here in Talavadi by 9 or 9:30am. Today, final preparations for the graduation and then tonight we will have the last of the house meetings which will mean I will have visited all 7 cell groups which are the 7 new churches.

5pm - After still no sign of Sharad's family, phone calls were made to the owner of the hired vehicle. In retaliation for the arrest last night, the road block is even worse now. No one can pass from either side of the state line and traffic is blocked for miles and miles. They cannot turn around and go back and they are not even half way here yet. We have been praying and expect a breakthrough.

6:40pm - They arrive here very hot and tired. The roadblock was suddenly removed. We are all very much glad to see them.

Tuesday, Sept. 17th -

5:15am - We all stayed up late and got up early this morning. Today at 10am is the students' graduation - then we will pick up and go back to Bangalore. The graduation got started late (10:45) because some of the invited people came by bus. The graduation service finished about 1pm then everybody stayed for lunch. We all prayed and left Talavadi at 3:30pm and arrived in Bangalore at 10pm, after a long, bumpy ride. I was looking forward to a good night's sleep, but barking dogs all night took care of that.

Wednesday, Sept. 18th -

6:45am - Up for the day. The dirty sooty air here makes the nose, the eyes, and throat sore. After breakfast, we hired a small van, took the three girls to school and went into the city to get my films developed, went to Campus Crusade for Christ to make a CD from the video, but we had to go to a music and film studio instead. We also stopped by Oasis Home for street kids where Grace works. Went to bed at 10pm knowing it's my last night here.

Thursday, Sept. 19th -

6:15am - Up for the day. There is nothing scheduled for today, so we'll all fellowship and I'll pack later. We'll leave here at 5:30pm for the airport.

7:15pm - I've just said goodbye to all of Sharad's family and came through security to the boarding gate area. We board at 8pm, depart 8:30pm for Bombay.

12:45am – I'm now in the boarding area for my flight to London at 2:15am. It took all this time to retrieve my luggage, take the shuttle bus to the international terminal, recheck it all again, go through customs/immigration, and so now it's a nice rest time. We left on time but got delayed in London because of some mechanical failure with the terminal stairs, so we lost an hour. But now it's 9:20am and my flight departure will be posted in 10 minutes then off to Boston. As on all the other flights, it was a smooth and sunny flight across the

Atlantic, arriving at Logan right on time. It was really wonderful to see Faith and the Skinners and we stopped for supper on the way home, arriving around 7:30pm. Wooo Hooo!!

Chapter 8
2003

Monday, Sept. 15th-

Another wonderful visit to India has begun. Bill will be picking me up at 8am for our drive to JFK. He actually arrived at 8:10 so that was good for Bill. Our drive to JFK was a time of good fellowship and a couple pit stops along the way. We missed a turn in NYC and ended up in New Jersey, but we had plenty of time to get back on course. We got stuck in a big traffic jam on the Whitestone Bridge, but still arrived at JFK at 2pm. We said goodbye, then I checked in my bags, went to the boarding area at waited for my flight at 5:45pm. It was right on time, and I arrived in Frankfurt 20 minutes early. A beautiful, smooth flight after we got above the clouds. We flew at 39,000 feet all the way. I got some Euro dollars and got a good breakfast, and I'm now waiting for the flight to Bangalore which leaves at 11:15am. **It is also now Tuesday the 16th** and a six hour time zone difference. The flight to Bangalore left exactly on time for the long final part, 10 hours and 20 minutes. We flew East over Hungary, Romania, Bulgaria, then turned south across the Black Sea, along the northern border of Turkey, then Iran and along the eastern coast of the Indian Ocean, and finally arriving in Bangalore at 11:59pm I.S.T. It was clear sky most of the way, and the visibility was excellent from 37,000 feet.

Sharad, Prema, Ruth, and Dominic met me at the airport. It was then another hour to their house. They gave me a very nice guest room with it's own bathroom, including sink and flush toilet. We stayed up until about 2am then slept until 8am. Now it's---

Wednesday, Sept. 17th-

I've been up for a while and already had breakfast and a bath. Then Sharad and I went into the city to cash some traveler's checks. Then we all just sat around the house resting and fellowship. Went to bed at 11:15pm and got up early today (**Thursday 18th**) for the long bumpy ride (7 hours) to Talavadi where we arrived at about 3:30pm. It's very warm but not hot like last year. We have many meetings arranged and I'll be here until next Wednesday. Along the way today, we stopped to encourage and pray for a new brother in Christ from only 6 months ago. He was a Hindu priest, and now he is so far the only Christian in his village. He has lost his job and much opposition and persecution from the others in his village, but now he is giving them tracts, books, and Bibles to read. He said before he confessed Christ, he knew the cost would be much for him and his wife, but now he knows Christ is the truth and he will gladly serve Him. Tonight we went to the church which has no place to meet except outside, sitting on the ground. This was my 3rd time here now and I can see how close the people have drawn together with me. There is such a strong bond of love which has knit our hearts together. The Word shared, prayer time, and the fellowship was very warm. I look forward to seeing these beloveds on Sunday when all of the churches come together and we share the Lord's Table together.

Friday, Sept. 19th-

After a good night's rest, ministry began right after breakfast. One brother (whom God had healed of AIDS when I was first here in 2001) had turned his back on the Lord, and went back to the world, came here to the house and wanted to repent and re-commit his life and service to the Lord. It was so wonderful to see how the love of God certainly does draw each of us to repentance and reconciliation. Tonight, we will go out to another village.

Saturday we will host a pastors/workers seminar for 3 hours, and perhaps another village meeting in the evening. On Sunday, there is a large hall arranged for our use. All 9 churches will come together. We fully expect a minimum of 300 people and a full day of ministry.

Saturday, Sept. 20th-

Last night's meeting in another village about 12km was also especially good. Since this is my 3rd time here, the people really have openly and lovingly received me. The ministry is very effective and people were prayed for. Many testified of being healed of various illnesses last year when they were prayed for.

Now it is nearing the hour of the pastors/wives meeting. The Lord has shown me last night to fast and pray for this meeting. We're expecting 30 - 35 pastors to come with their wives also. The theme will be **"Issues of the Heart"** to deal with 3 key areas to focus on: **Strife, Competitive Spirit, and Pride.** This will be a very different format than is usually presented. The meeting went very well, but only 7 pastors came and one brought his wife. Those who came were sincere about working together and no longer working/speaking against each other. There was much forgiveness and then we washed all their feet. Later, I was taken to the gypsy camp. I love to go there. They are always so appreciative that anyone would visit them. One is beaten by her father nearly everyday to make her renounce Christ. She refuses, and was beaten just before we arrived. A photo was taken to constantly remind me to pray for her and her family's salvation.

Sunday, September 21st-

It doesn't seem like the first week has already gone by. Today, all 9 nine churches and cell groups are coming together. We have rented a large hall. For ministry we'll have communion together and then prayer for each of the people who want prayer. This turned out to be a very large meeting. People came as far away as 60km. About 200 people as close as a count as could be taken and then 1 on 1 prayer after took another hour and a half. Then they were served lunch and sent home. We provided their lunch and bus fare home. Then we had a couple hours rest but people kept coming here for prayer, so all day we were busy. We went to the village tonight with the new cell group. The meeting started with about 30 people but ended up with nearly 100. The room filled up, then the small patio, then the street in front of the house. Prayer took about an hour more by the time the last person was prayed for. So it was a very long busy day, but very fruitful. We are already getting reports back from the villages of many people who got healed. They tell everybody so the crowds continue to grow. They want me to come back next year and have a large crusade. We'll have to wait on the Lord about that.

Monday, Sept. 22nd-

I finally got to sleep about 12:30 last night. The anointing and excitement of the day kept us all up late. But now it's 7am and about 9am some people are coming here for teaching of the Word until 1pm for the next 3 days. Then later today, we are going to the other new cell group and to the forest village where God healed the boy born crippled and could not walk.

*A note about the rats!! When I came here the first time, there were rats running anywhere they desired, including on me in my bed. I wrote of this in my journal of the first trip. I rebuked the rats at that time and did not see anymore after that. Last year when I came on my

2nd trip here, I also saw no rats, but Sharad told me yesterday that his workers found two dead rats on the tile roof directly over where I had slept. No one has ever found any reason why 2 rats would climb up onto the roof and then die right on this particular part of the roof, or why two perfectly healthy rats would die on the roof in the first place.

People began to come by the house for prayer and the Word and this continued all day. Also, 3 people wanted to be water baptized including a former Hindu man and his wife. So we took them out in the countryside to an old quarry where the elephants come for water. All the streams and rivers are still completely dried up for 2 years now. After the baptisms, we came back to the house and recorded a video of some testimonies. One was the gypsy girl who is beaten nearly everyday by her father; the other 2 were the Hindu man and his wife. We will take this video to Bangalore on Wednesday and put it on CD. Also, during the day, 2 men came by and wanted us to hold a big meeting in their village on Wednesday, but we won't have time. We'll be leaving here late morning. We never did get to the meeting that was set for tonight. It's been re-scheduled for tomorrow.

Tuesday, Sept. 23rd-

Today we expect people again to come here. So we'll wait on the Lord for His will. As we are having breakfast, the Hindu couple came by to say goodbye and for prayer. They live about 40k from here. We'll be passing through their village on the way back to Bangalore. We stopped at their house last week on the way here, and they stayed for all the meetings here in Talavadi area. Now we are going to watch the video from the testimonies. The Hindu photographer who took all the pictures of our first meeting did the video taping. We will edit it and put it on a CD in Bangalore. Both meetings tonight were, once again, a great outpouring of God's love and compassion. The first meeting was held at the home of a farmer. His house was completely a thatched hut, but lots of room inside. After we prayed for all the people, he took me into the pasture to pray for his cow because every time he milks her, she kicks him and spills the milk pail. He wanted me to lay hands on the cow's head. She didn't like that, but she soon settled down. Then the last meeting started with about 30 people and ended up with close to 100. When we start praying for the people, others seem to come out of nowhere and they too, want prayer. So now the Talavadi ministry for me is finished and we will begin our seven hour drive to Bangalore in the mid morning (10 -10:30).

Wednesday, Sept. 24th-

A very noisy morning. The man on the loud speaker at the mosque got all the dogs barking and howling at 5:15 am, so none of us could sleep even until 6. I'm already packed for our long trip back to Bangalore. We expect to arrive there about 5 or 5:30pm. We had breakfast by 7:30 and people came on early buses from as far away as 40k (24miles) for prayer and to say goodbye.

This kind of love, commitment, and caring is so humbling that I can't even begin to describe it in any words that I know of, except to bow before the Lord in such gratefulness and thanksgiving for the hearts of such people as this. People kept coming right up until we left at 10:45. Their hunger for more of God's touch is why leaving here is always such a heart- ripping time of the ministry here.

It was a long, hot ride back to Bangalore, but we arrived about 5:30pm. I went to the cybershop to send e-mails home, but they would not go, so I'll try again in the morning. After a hot bath and good supper, I went to bed around 9:15 and slept until 6:45am.

Thursday, Sept, 25th-

It's now just before 10am and Sharad and I will be going to send the e-mails again, and then we have some things to do in the city: getting traveler's checks cashed, photos printed, video put over on CD, etc. so we'll have a busy time today. We ran into a few difficulties with the video and spent all evening working on the final version. It's now 11pm and we're having supper just now.

Friday, Sept. 26th-

Today early (9am) I will go to the cybershop and send new e-mails, then we have an appointment at 11 at the video studio to review the video before it goes onto CD's. We also have to pick up all our pictures from the photo lab. Today is Elisabeth's birthday, so we'll have some cake and goodies later. Also tonight, there will be a home meeting - Word and prayer. This will be my last night to spend overnight. Tomorrow the computer tech will be coming to repair Sharad's computer. Then he'll begin to translate and print the Bible studies into Kannada language.

Saturday, Sept. 27th-

Yesterday, we finished all ministry- related duties and enjoyed the rest of the evening together. I had about $200 left over from all the money given, so I took Sharad and Prema to a local furniture store to buy 2 new beds: 1 for them and one for one of the girls. These three have been sleeping on the hard floor for nearly 7 months with no bed. I couldn't in all good conscience just close my eyes to this need, and was so excited about finding good beds for such a low cost. So now, they will all have good sleeping from now on.

Today is my last day. Grace is taking me to a small shop to buy some gifts for home. Other than that, we'll all just spend the day together. I'll send one last e-mail home later, and then around 10pm we'll leave for the airport. My flight leaves at 1:50am.

The ride to the airport was fun. The whole family packed into the van and off we went. I left from a different terminal this time; they couldn't come inside so we had to say quick goodbyes. Security was tight and the customs/immigration line was long. It took about one hour and 45 minutes to get through, so that took up all the waiting time. In 15 minutes we boarded the aircraft. As we were taxiing for takeoff, a strange thumping noise was coming from the baggage area, so we went back to the terminal. They unloaded all of the baggage and rearranged it. We soon departed and did not hear anymore strange noises coming from under our feet!! The entire process cost us only a one hour delay, but no other problem. We made up most of that time by the time we got to Frankfurt. That flight left right on time. The flight across the Atlantic was cloudy all the way to JFK where it was raining. Bill was waiting for me at ground transportation. We stopped in Connecticut for Pizza and I got home at about 7:15pm, tired and ready for a hot shower and a nice soft bed.

Chapter Nine
2004

Tuesday, Sept. 20th -

God has proven Himself so faithful to me again. When I became aware that the Lord would have me go this year, I released my faith for the necessary provisions and began to prepare in July for this next trip to India. I found an excellent flight schedule and a very good price as well. I'm leaving on Wednesday the 22nd with Simon picking me up at 10am for the 5 hour drive to JFK. All the funding has been excellent, including a laptop for Sharad. Last minute preparations include getting my Traveler's checks and packing tomorrow. At 5pm I am the Guest Speaker at the F.G.B.M.F.I Chapter in Keene tomorrow night, and then comes the "big day" of long hours with very little sleep, but worth every minute.

Wednesday, Sept. 22nd -

2:45pm - I'm now in the boarding gate area for my flight at 5:35pm. The ride with Simon was wonderful and we were here at JFK in just 4 hours on the Merimar Parkway in Connecticut. 1 hour in the line to get my suitcases checked in, security took less than 1 minute including the laptop. It's a beautiful, clear, warm sunny day - perfect for flying......

3:30pm - Our plane has arrived at the JFK Lufthansa terminal - it is an airbus 340 - 300. It is being cleaned and serviced and we'll begin boarding at 4:50pm

Thursday, Sept. 23rd-

7:40am, and here I am in Frankfurt, Germany, after a very smooth flight from JFK. The plane took a more northerly route; up over Connecticut, Massachusetts, Manchester, NH, up over Maine and just to the south of Greenland and Iceland. We flew over Scotland and then south across England and into Germany. We descended down through 3 layers of clouds, and found it rainy here and 54 degrees. My next flight leaves here at 10:40am, so I'm enjoying a cup of coffee in a little café here at the airport.

An 11am computer crash at the terminal prevented us from leaving on time, but we were finally out by noon. It was an excellent, but long flight (10 hours) to Bangalore. We made up all the lost time and arrived on time. After about an hour and a half for immigration and customs, baggage claim, I left with Sharad, Prema, Grace and Hannah. We stayed up and had tea and fellowship until 2:30am. Then I slept until 7am. Today we will send e-mails home, cash traveler's checks, get supplies, and drive to Talavadi (7hours).

Friday, Sept. 24th-

At 10pm we finally arrived at Talavadi. It rained most of the way and much of the road is washed away and we could only drive 25 to 30mph and less in some places. We had supper and then tried to get internet and e-mail installed into the laptop, but unsuccessful. It's midnight now and we are all very tired and ready for bed.

Saturday, Sept. 25th-

6:40am- Up for the day. I don't know what the plan for today is yet. It is still raining very steadily. I think we will work with the computer. Sharad bought 10 hours of service on a CD, so once it is installed we should be able to use it here in Talavadi for e-mail.

The Bible school students came at 10:15 and we had class until 12:45pm. I taught on having a vision for our lives and will continue that on Monday or until finished. Then we had lunch, tried to get the internet to work, but could not. Later in the evening we went to the village where the church meets outside. There were twice as many people this time than last year. A super time of ministry and many received from the Lord what they needed.

Sunday, Sept. 26th-

Ministry during the morning service included praying for adults, as well as for all the children. After church we had tea and went to a nearby cybershop to send e-mails home. We came in Dominic's van. He let us use it for the whole time in Talavadi area. We ate lunch about 2:30 – then had some rest time. At 5:30 we are going to another village cell group about 25k from here. It will take 1 ½ hours because the roads are so bad. When we arrived, lightening was beginning to light up the sky all around us. The house was filled with people and others were outside that could not get in because there was no room.

This was the place last year I had prayed for a young boy who needed a new kidney; but not anymore. God completely healed him and I saw and spoke with him tonight. After all the people were prayed for, we stayed for coffee and crackers. We all got soaked leaving - it was raining very hard like a Florida thunderstorm. After coming home, we had supper and Sharad and I tried to get the internet CD to work. After reviewing all the connection procedures, we discovered that the Talavadi phone lines are so old that they are not equipped to be able to carry internet service. So we'll just use the old CD in Bangalore instead of the cybershop.

Monday, Sept. 27th-

It's chilly, damp and cloudy and looks like it will rain again. The monsoon season is continuing longer this year and has ended the 2 year drought. Today, I'll teach in the Bible school from 10am till 1pm and hopefully finish the "vision" teaching.

I didn't finish, we simply ran out of time. We left this afternoon to go to the gypsy village. It is far from here and takes1 ½ hours to get there. After that, we went to another village where cell group #10 has been established. It is very good to see the growth of the Christian community here. It rained again and on the way home, our driver took a wrong turn, and we got lost. It took us until 11pm before we got home.

Tuesday, Sept. 28th-

It's cool and cloudy again this morning. We all slept a little later, but not much. The noise of the village waking up keeps us from sleeping much later - the chickens, roosters, crows, all are very loud, plus the Muslim Mosque at 5am with the loudspeakers. I finished the "vision" teaching in the Bible school today. Tonight, we went to a new village where cell group #11 has been established. Once again, we witnessed a great outpouring of God's Spirit of mercy and compassion upon the people. It had rained most of the day and early evening, but it didn't stop the people from coming.

Wednesday, Sept. 29th-

Cloudy, cool again. Sharad and Prema are cold and we are all wearing coats/sweaters. It just feels cool to me at 55F to 60F. That's about 25 degrees below where it should be.

Today, I'll start teaching agape love of God from 1 Corinthians 13. We finished the class a little early so we could go to a nearby village to get the graduation certificates printed, and send some e-mails.

Tonight's village meeting was awesome. Every person in the house wanted to be baptized in the Holy Spirit. He came upon all of us so powerfully, and we all got shaky and could hardly stand; like we were all drunk. After we came home from the meeting, we were up late because none of us could sleep. I was awake at 4:30am.

Thursday, Sept. 30th-

Cool, but the sun is coming up. Jeremiah's birthday is today - 20 years old!!!

My time here is drawing near to the end now. Only today and tomorrow and the Bible school classes will be finished. We have 14 students graduating. There are two more village meetings scheduled; one for tonight and one for tomorrow night, the open air crusade on Saturday, water baptisms late Saturday afternoon, Sunday morning service, then back to Bangalore. I finished the **"Love of God"** series today. The cell group meeting got cancelled because of a big rainstorm which caused the river to overflow and washed out the road. The electric was out for about 9 hours, so we sat in the dark with one candle and had bible study and fellowship. We all went to bed early but then the Muslims in the Mosque near us began preaching and screaming through their loudspeakers until nearly 12:30am. Sharad knows their language and said it was a declaration of Holy War against America and a call to rise up to kill any American anywhere. When Sharad heard that, he and George got the motor bike ready to take me away quickly if anyone came to the house. No one did, and finally, after all the noise stopped, we were able to get a few hours sleep before the daily Muslim call to prayer at 4:45am.

Friday, Oct. 1st-

This morning we are all very tired and sleepy after last night's Muslim uprising. Today, our Bible school will be finished. After completing the **"Love of God"** yesterday, today we will have communion followed by foot washing, and then we will have the graduation. Tonight we will have the last cell group meeting. Tomorrow, we are still hopeful of the one big crusade meeting. Some of the local pastors have stirred up so much trouble that we have already lost the first place for the meeting. Today, we will find out if the second place is still available. Word came during the foot-washing that we were denied the second place, so we'll have the meeting here. We can hold about 300 people, so we'll make do. The rest of the foot-washing finished and then we held the graduation service for the students. Three of them had to go early because someone died in their village. Later in the evening, we did the last cell group meeting for this time that I was here. It was a very joyful time of celebration. All those people remember me and asked about my family. A Hindu temple man came, played his keyboard with us and got saved along with one other person. We celebrated because we lost the second place to hold Saturday's meeting. All these villagers have seen and have experienced for themselves the great move of God, so when some of the local pastors tried to stop us, it caused us to celebrate even more. It began to rain hard about 8pm and it took a long time to get home. It was still raining at 11pm when I went to bed. A big rat was also killed. He came in the house when we did because there was so much flooding of the street outside.

Saturday, October 2nd-

Early this morning we are preparing this house to hold the large meeting. We'll start about 10:30 with tea right after everyone is here by bus or walking. We expect no less than 3 or 4 hundred people from 12 villages. I imagine it will take along time to pray for all of them, but that's what they don't get anywhere else. That's one of the reasons other pastors are so jealous. They preach in nearly empty church buildings, and we have hundreds every year. Our afternoon officially started at 10:30 but the gypsy church arrived on an early bus at 9:15am. There was a steady flow of people from that time on. By the time we started, there were 320 counted inside the house and many more outside and more still arriving after we started. We made a video of the entire program including the 2 hours it took to pray for all the people. We then had a quick cup of tea, light lunch and to the river to baptize two new believers. After that, we went 30 kilometers from here to videotape a young girl's testimony. She came two years ago with huge boils all over her body. She was twelve years old then. After anointing her with oil and prayer, she was miraculously healed. Her skin is so smooth and beautiful you would never know she ever had this problem. Her parents were so excited to talk about this, even on the videotape. They said three other people in their village also received healing from anointing the same meeting. There is going to be a public release of this testimony coming out in a local magazine later this year. We then prayed for five people in the house there and got home about 8:30. It was a long day. I went to bed right after supper. We have another long day tomorrow.

Sunday, October 3rd-
Loud music at 5am to celebrate a wedding woke us all up. We will have to pack, eat breakfast, have a short time of worship/prayer and leave Talavadi at 9:30 for the 7 hour drive back to Bangalore, hopefully arriving around 4:30. I've been scheduled to speak at Dominic's church at 6pm, so we don't have much time to spare. I have to wear my "city clothes" including a tie for this meeting. We arrived in Bangalore at 4:45 pm. Sharad's daughters had hot water for a quick refreshing bath, a cup of tea, and off I went to church, experiencing a very wonderful time there. Dominic asked me to serve the communion and then the Word, and then pray for all those who wanted prayer (so everyone came for prayer). We got home about 9pm, had supper, fellowshipped for a while, then I went to bed at 11pm - a long day.

Monday, October 4th-
7:15am- Dominic is coming at 8am to take me to his flat for breakfast. He arrived at 8:15 and we had a great time of fellowship. He brought me back to Sharad's about 9:45 then Sharad and I went to the cybershop to check and send e-mail. From there, we went to get the video put onto CDs. That took a long time. We had lunch, then I loaded the digital camera photos onto the laptop, and Grace and I went to a small shop to do a little shopping. After supper, we had a little more time to visit, had a hot bath, finished packing and left about 9:15pm for the airport. I'm here now in the boarding area. All went very fast through security/immigration. Now it's about 2 hours before flight time, so I'll just rest.

Tuesday, October 5th-
It's 8am, Germany time and I'm sitting in the boarding area. We start to board at 9am. It was a very nice, smooth flight from Bangalore and I actually got four or five hours of sleep after dinner. Here in Frankfurt, it is reasonably warm and partly sunny. I'm comfortable in

my short sleeve shirt. I'm looking forward to seeing Bill and Ghing at JFK this afternoon. My flight left right on time and I was amazed how fast I went through immigration/customs at JFK. From the time I left the plane, 20 minutes later, I was in Bill's vehicle!! Even my suitcase was one of the first off the plane, I was 1st at customs, and done so soon. Now, all the "after trip" things to do and another successful time of ministry finished for this year.

Chapter Ten
2005

Thursday, Sept. 21st, 2005 –

God has been so faithful and wonderful to me again, providing another opportunity to go to India for the 5th time. Funding was provided in great abundance and now I've begun the long journey. Simon picked me up at 9:45am and we stopped for lunch and now it is 2:20pm. I'm already at JFK, gone through check- in, security, and sitting in the gate area!!! What a fast, efficient time this was. We board at 5pm, so I've sure got plenty of time to spare. My flight leaves at 5:50pm, arriving in Frankfurt, Germany at 7:30am Friday Germany time.

Friday, Sept. 22nd-

It is now 8:10am and I'm sitting in the boarding area for the 10 hour flight to Bangalore. The flight from N.Y. to here was on time and an excellent flight, as have been all the previous flights. The meals were great, I got a little sleep, and now I'll be here for 3 more hours. The flight to Bangalore was on time, and long, 10 hours, but I arrived to find Sharad , Prema and Grace waiting for me. We came back to the house, drank tea and fellowshipped until about 3:30am. I went to bed and got 3 hours of sleep. The other daughters will be up soon for school. They're having exams today, so they want me to pray with them. They are very delighted with the Hershey candies I brought them.

Saturday, Sept. 24th-

After tea and breakfast, Sharad and I spent the whole day in Bangalore shopping for a new computer and printer. We finally found one at an excellent price, after going to four or five different places. It took quite a while to have all the software and drivers installed, and then the tech came home with us and set it all up. Then we took him home about 10:15pm. Hannah and I played solitaire on the computer until around 11:15, then a hot bath and to bed.

Sunday, Sept. 25th-

Sharad and I had breakfast and fellowship again early this morning. A work crew came to install the phone line for free internet service. It should be ready for use sometime on Monday. Grace took me to the cybershop to check and send e-mail. I rested awhile and at 4:15 Dominic came to take me to his church to do the service tonight. He has a small congregation of about 22 but very faithful to him. Most of them are young and filled with zeal for the Lord. We had communion and then I spoke about faithfulness and then ended with prayer for those who wanted.

Monday, Sept. 26th-

Today is Elizabeth's 16th birthday. Sharad and I went into the city for about 3 hours, had lunch at KFC and came home. We finished our discussion about George and Barnabas and the plans for meetings in Talavadi. Later, the whole family including Dominic, Joy and Joel went to KFC/Pizza Hut for supper together to celebrate Elizabeth's birthday. The wait staff told everybody in the restaurant to stop eating and sing "Happy Birthday" with them. After supper, we came home and had chocolate cake and tea. We went to bed early so we could get up at 4am to pack and leave for Talavadi.

Tuesday, Sept. 27th-

We got up at 4am, packed and left at 5:20 for Talavadi. We drove until Mysore, stopping there for breakfast. Then we went to a house there to pray for 4 people (1 with cancer), continuing on to Talavadi, arriving around 2:30pm. Sharad was excited to show me the new bathroom for my room. It is very nice with tiled walls and floor, flush toilet, hot and cold water. The plumber is returning tomorrow to finish the connections for the water and water heater, and then it will be finished. We had a late lunch and unpacked, took a short nap to rest. The power went out until 9pm from 3:30. So we had supper by candlelight and went to bed around 10pm.

Wednesday, Sept. 28th-

I got up at 6:30. Sharad and I had tea together in my room. We will be meeting with George and Barnabas at 8:30. It seems they don't want to carry on with the churches and new cell groups, so we need to see how this work can be restored. Our meeting lasted 4 ½ hours and we believe a breakthrough has occurred. We will be going tonight for the first meeting. This is one of the 3 new cell groups that I didn't have time to visit last year. The meeting was excellent with about 11 people from a completely all Hindu village, but these 11 were all recently born again (1 year). One of the saddest was a young couple who had just lost their 6 month old son. He got sick and died. But after prayer, we believed God together to bring comfort and healing. After the meeting, a very heavy thunderstorm came and we drove home. It took an hour to go only 10km or about six miles. The road was horrible to begin with, but the rain and darkness made it nearly impossible to tell where all the holes were. After supper at 8:30, we went to Pastor Rubin's house. I met him last year at the seminar. His wife had been very sick for nearly 3 weeks, so we went to pray for her. When we got to their house, we found out they had no food and they had nothing to eat for more than a week, including their 2 children. We prayed for them and then gave them money for food.

Thursday, Sept. 29th-

Today I will be teaching the village workers from the Bible study workbook **"Introduction",** so they can learn how to teach the new believers. Two problems had been that most in the villages cannot read, and most have only candles for after dark. We didn't have the original in English so we used 1 John. It went so well that Sharad and the others want me to do the whole book with them and they are inviting others to come.

Tonight we went to one of the nine churches where I have gone from the beginning (4 times). It's so good to see how they have grown from only a few to nearly 60 over the last 5 years. As always, there were many to pray for. Many wanted prayer for headaches and body pain. Many of the children asked for prayer to stop grinding their teeth at night.

Friday, Sept. 30th-

Today is Jeremiah's 21st birthday ; a day very big in my life as a dad. (I was here last year on this date as well when he turned twenty. To have such a son who has served and honored the Lord since he was 4 years old; and continues to be faithful, loyal, loving, and giving is a son who brings great joy. Sharad's wife bought a birthday cake, had it decorated, even with two candles in the shape of #21. All of us (Sharad, Prema, the 4 workers and myself), lit the candles, sang "Happy Birthday" then cut and ate the cake. It was a very special time since I've been away form home nine days already and could not be there. Then I continued to teach the workers from 1 John Bible study workbook that they will be teaching in the villages. Also, today, I took first real shower in the 5 times I've come to India. What a blessing!!! The water is pumped into a large holding tank and heated by the sun. The water is then gravity fed into the kitchen and bathroom. So now I have a beautiful bathroom including tile walls and floor, shower, sink, and toilet. I think "Wow, now anyone I bring would be comfortable." The water is not hot, but very warm, so it feels refreshing. They also bought me a very nice new mattress for the new cot they had made. So I'm very happy to enjoy these things. Tonight, we are going to the village where many of the miracle healings occurred in 2001, including the old man who had lain crippled for two years on a mat, and God completely restored him overnight.

The meeting tonight was held in a Hindu house but they invited us there for the meeting. Many people came and so many prayed for; including one man who wanted to be saved and delivered from alcohol. We stayed awhile after because tea, coffee, and cookies were prepared for us.

Saturday, Oct. 1st-

After breakfast, we again gathered together for an hour in the Bible study workbook. Then Sharad, Prema, and I went to the nearby city (15miles)to check e-mail and get some new batteries for Jeremiah's digital camera. The roads are so bad that it takes one hour each way to go the 15 miles. That would be like going all the way to Rutland or Keene just to check e-mails. When we got there we found only a few shops open - all the rest closed due to a strike to protest a new road being built. We did find one open cybershop and only after reading two e-mails and answering them, the internet connection was lost and could not be restored so we will go back on Monday to try again. The electric goes out at least twice a day still here for three to four hours at a time. We'll be going to another one of the new cell groups in about an hour, and looking forward to going. The road was terrible, mostly huge holes and washouts. There are still two groups that we can't get to because the roads washed out in the thunderstorm we got earlier in the week. Tonight's meeting was well attended and I saw many familiar faces. As usual, they all wanted prayer.

Sunday, Oct. 2nd-

Barnabas will have all the street kids (about 120) for Sunday School from 8:30 - 9:30 and then we will have the regular church service from 10-11:30. We have to be finished by then for the people to catch their respective village buses home. The service was excellent - several different people gave testimony of answered prayer. We had communion. Right after the service a young man wanted to be saved. So now we have eight for baptisms on Wednesday. We'll be going to the dam where I went the first year here. We went quite far tonight to another one of the churches. Once again, the roads were awful, but the meeting was very good. It was the village where God healed the young boy who was born unable to walk.

Monday, Oct. 3rd-

Today we'll resume the Bible study workbook on 1 John until around 11am. Then we're going back to the city to send e-mails. The strike was only for Saturday so things should be back to normal. Later, we are going either to the distant forest village or to the gypsy church. It will be decided this morning. Turns out, it will be the gypsy church. It's nearly two hours away because of the road conditions. We are still using Dominic's van, but I think we are going to hire a 4 wheeler for this particular trip. Today, we've already broken the tailpipe/muffler, one wheel, and the fuel line and had to pay for these repairs - now I can see why God supplied extra money this time.

Heavy thunderstorms have washed out the road, so no gypsy camp trip tonight. Instead, we've been invited to a house meeting in a nearby village, and after that our Hindu driver wants us to come pray for his wife. So we're having tea now and we'll be leaving around 5:30pm. This meeting was awesome and the house was jammed full. I still don't see how so many people can fit into a room, but they do.

Many prayed for and one woman with a demon for six years was set free. What an exciting moment!! First she cried, and then she laughed and laughed. The sickness in her lungs also left immediately with the demon. Her whole family is now rejoicing together. No one had been able to help her, and so she had been like this for those six years. By the time we all got home, our driver went somewhere else, so I guess we'll be praying for his wife tomorrow.

Tuesday, Oct. 4th-

Today we will be having a large meeting here, starting with the Children's Program. We expect a minimum of 100 people. We know there will probably be more. It's now 9:30 and people are already arriving by buses from the surrounding villages. We'll start around 10:30. We have rented a pandal for outside to cover chairs and tables for the people to have lunch after. We have hired a cook to prepare the meal and he has already started. The meeting turned out well with about 150 people all jammed into one room; as the video will show. It took nearly 1 ½ hours to pray for everyone who wanted prayer, but I'm very used to that. Later in the evening, we visited another of the new cell groups. That house also was filled to the walls. We made another video of the meeting.

Wednesday, Oct. 5th-

This morning we are going to set up a display of all the Bible study workbooks that have been translated and printed. We want to send a CD to G.Y.E. to thank them for their gift to help cover the costs. So we will do a little short filming for that and **"Teaching the Teachers".** Then we'll be filming a short documentary on Talavadi and what it looks like here, followed by water baptisms after that. There may be one more cell group tonight, but not confirmed, then early to bed. We're leaving around 4:30 am to get back to Bangalore.

We decided to do the Talavadi video first so we could film all the animals along the road in the morning. We spent several hours filming, and then we met the 3 people for baptism. We took them to a river and before baptism, we slid in the waterfalls and swam and just had some fun. After the baptisms, we came back to the house for lunch. It was around 2pm. The cameraman and driver have gone out to finish the documentary. We are now setting up for the G.Y.E. books and we'll be ready when the cameraman returns. We are not going to the meeting tonight. It is the same group we started with last week. Instead, we are going to pack everything and go to bed early for our long trip tomorrow.

Thursday, Oct. 6th-

We woke at about 4:15am and we loaded the van and were on the road at 5am. We stopped at 7:30 in Mysore for breakfast and rest, and then we continued nonstop to Bangalore. It takes another 1 ½ hours to get through most of Bangalore to Sharad's house. We got here about 1:15pm, had lunch and fellowship and later, a hot bath, supper and bed at 10pm.

Friday, Oct. 7th-

Up at 6:30 and had tea and fellowship until around 9:30 - now we're going into the city for changing currency and the videos to be put on CDs. That will take several hours at a film studio, but we do it each year, so it is routine. We left the films, came home for lunch, and went back around 5pm. We brought the "new" DVDs home to look at on the computer. The quality is excellent and we enjoyed watching them which took until 10:30pm.

Saturday, Oct. 8th-

Everyone but me is sleeping late this morning. It's already 7:30 and no one is up yet. Later after breakfast, Grace is taking me to a few local shops for personal items to bring home. We were in the city for a few hours, so we went to KFC for lunch too. I still had some small amount of money left in rupees, so I took all of the family to supper at KFC. It rained very hard all evening, flooding some of the low-lying roads. It continued to rain steady for most of the night.

Sunday, Oct. 9th-

Up at 7am. I had tea with Sharad and then breakfast. The rain has stopped, but it still cloudy. I checked some e-mail and sent one home, checked weather for Monday night in Bangalore, Tuesday morning in Frankfurt, Tuesday midday in NYC. Things look favorable for timely flying. We went into the city for awhile today, got caught in a two hour downpour and got soaking wet. At least it's tropical here, so the rain wasn't too cold. I did the evening service at Dominic's church, and then we all stayed up until 11pm.

Monday, Oct. 10th-

Up at 6am, I thought I might sleep a little longer, but the excitement of going home must have made me wake up sooner than usual. After breakfast, we are going into town to see if we can find "Keyman" language software CD to bring back to Vermont. Then Sharad can send the translated study books by e-mail and I can print them right at home, avoiding costly shipping by mail which sometimes takes up to two weeks. Later today my desire is to have a hot bath, a couple hours nap, and final packing. We'll leave around 10pm for the airport, arriving by 11pm. We left at 10:10pm and got to the airport about 10:45pm. Check-in/security was smooth and fast. It's only 11:15 so I have 3 more hours to wait, but at least I'm in the boarding area which is really crowded. There are two other flights leaving from the gate before mine.

Tuesday, Oct. 11th-

Frankfurt- Well, here I am in Frankfurt, Germany at 8:15 am - all checked through security and sitting in the boarding area. I should have only about one hour to wait for the flight to JFK (8 hours). The flight from Bangalore was glass smooth all the way, and here in Frankfurt, it's a cool 50 degrees and sunny.

My flight back to JFK was without incident and John M. and Dan C. were there to greet me and drive me home, arriving about 6pm.

Chapter Eleven
2007

Tuesday, Feb. 6th 2007 -

It hardly seems possible, but here again is the favor of God to bless me with another opportunity to go for the 6th trip to South India. All finances have come in full abundance; some expected, some just over the last 2 days. This year's flight times have changed a bit. I'm not leaving JFK until 9:25pm tonight. That will cut out most of the layover time in Frankfurt. Simon is picking me up at noon for our ride to JFK, and I'll have much time there before departure. It was a very great ride and time of fellowship with Simon. We left Chester at noon and arrived at JFK right after 4pm. Check-in and security was very quick/smooth, and at 4:15 I'm already in my gate area, with lots of time to wait.

Wednesday, Feb. 7th-

The flight from JFK was exactly on time and a very smooth crossing of the ocean. We were served a nice dinner at around 11pm over St. John's Island as we flew over the northeast coastline. A delicious sunrise breakfast was served as we flew along the southern coast of Wales and England. We continued on across the English Channel, Belgium, and on to Germany arriving in Frankfurt at 11:05am. The shuttle buses were waiting for the plane and a quick transfer soon occurred to take us to the terminal. I had to walk only one gate for the boarding area for the long flight to Bangalore. The wait was only 20 minutes before boarding the huge 747 jumbo jet. This part of the trip was a different route. We flew south across the Alps which were spectacular in the glistening midday sun shining on the snow-covered peaks above the clouds. We continued our flight on across northern Greece, and then crossed the Black Sea onward over Istanbul, Turkey. Once again, I was looking down on miles and miles of the high, snow-covered mountains of eastern Turkey. As we crossed the southeast coastline of Turkey, we were briefly over the northeast corner of the Mediterranean Sea and crossed over the coast of Lebanon. We crossed over Syria and Iraq as well. It began to get dark as the plane took a more southerly turn which took us the entire length of the Saudi Arabian Peninsula. As we neared the southern end, we flew directly over the port city of Dubai on the Persian Gulf. This city had the appearance of spectacular sparkling diamonds clustered together in the otherwise completely black desert terrain beneath the starlit sky. We turned east, crossing the Arabian Sea, and on to the northern coastline of India. We flew south along the coastline, finally turning inland for our arrival at Bangalore at exactly 1:15am, right on time. I have never flown on any airline which keeps such an excellent schedule as does Lufthansa.

Thursday, Feb. 8th-

1:15am **-** It took only an amazing half an hour to deplane, go through immigration, baggage claim, and customs and I was outside in the warm 78 degree temperature. Sharad, Prema, and Grace were waiting and we all came back to their house for tea and fellowship until 3am. I noticed right away that my feet were not swollen even the tiniest amount as they had been in previous years from such long distance flying at high altitudes.

I had a refreshing little short nap until 7:45am. I was up and wide awake to greet Sharad's other daughters as they were getting ready for school. We prayed together and then had breakfast and more fellowship. Then we went into the center of the city to cash my travelers' checks, went to a card shop, to the post office, and finally returning to the house for lunch. Oh it was so good to once again enjoy the rich flavorful currie chicken, rice and veggies. We all took a short rest until 4:30pm. So far, I don't even feel tired or any jet lag at all, after just flying nearly 11,000 miles and crossing 10.5 hours of time zones. Grace and I then walked to a new international coffee house where we indulged in a hot, big cup of Columbian coffee. She wanted to tell me about the man she had met who fulfilled exactly a prophecy I had told her in 2004, even to the small scar on his face. This was very exciting news as I believe there will be a wedding within the next year. We came home and had supper and fellowship until 10:30pm and went to bed, never even feeling any effects of the long journey.

Friday, Feb. 9th-

6am**-** I woke up at 5:30am so well rested that I couldn't sleep any longer. Today we are going to Talavadi. I don't know the time yet, but it is a long, bumpy 7 hour ride. We do it every year so I'm certainly ready. As I'm writing, I hear kitchen noises from my bedroom door, so I know tea will soon be ready. I have a very nice room including a western style flush toilet!!! What a difference six years has made!!!

*We just found out that we cannot go to Talavadi today because of a farmers strike over water rights to the river which flows from Karnataka into Tamil Nadu. They have totally blocked the highway and allowing no vehicles to pass. So we'll stay here another day. There is another much longer and more remote road and we will get up at 3:30am and leave at 4:30am.

Saturday, Feb. 10th-

It is 4am and our vehicle should be here shortly for loading all the supplies we got yesterday, and then we will leave for Talavadi.

Our driver showed up late (5:15). He was a Muslim and became rude and angry when he discovered we are Christians, but he had very good driving skills and arrived in Talavadi in 5½ hours. After a short rest, we went to dedicate 3 acres of beautiful new land overlooking the Nilgiri Mountains to the east, and donated for a church and Bible school. After returning to the house, several people came by for prayer. Then we had lunch and laid down our tired bodies to sleep for a couple hours. I have the same room again this year with the new bathroom.

After having tea, we went 30km to a village to visit the young girl whom God healed of boils all over her body. We had great fellowship and prayed for her education, her father's continued good health, her mom's elbow, and for her brother's job and that he would continue to be faithful to the Lord. Then we were served hot milk flavored with ginger. We left soon after for the long, bumpy ride back to Talavadi. Supper and fellowship with George and Barnabas followed. Both of them had repented of trying to undermine and overthrow the ministry last summer. There was prayer and forgiveness and now we can work together as one again.

Sunday, Feb. 11th-

I woke up at 5am because of the loudspeakers in the mosque. Today back home, Tom and Carol will be doing the Sunday service in my place. Jeremiah will be leaving at noon for Texas for 5 days, so Faith will be alone all this week. Here, we will also be having Sunday service around 9:30. There were only about ten people in attendance but some of them I've known for 4 years, including the farmer whose cow I prayed for, and the Hindu priest and his wife whom I met four years back and baptized them in the "elephant pond". After service we had lunch and fellowship, then a short nap/rest. At 5:30 we went to the distant forest village where there are only 8 houses. It's so good to see all these people again. We've been going every year for 6 years now. This area is so remote that the people are like society's forgotten ones, but certainly not by the Lord. He manifested Himself through powerful signs and wonders, just as He has always done, touching and healing people of their infirmities. This is also the same village where God healed a young crippled boy who could not walk since birth. I saw him again tonight and he looks great, still running and playing with his friends. We came back late, had supper and fellowshipped until 11pm. We were all very tired and ready for bed. It's been very comfortable temperatures everyday - about 86 F daytime and 58Fnight time which is good for sleeping.

Monday, Feb. 12th-

Another beautiful morning - the birds are chirping, the roosters are crowing, the sun is coming up and it feels just like a mid-summer morning in Vermont. After breakfast, I did a two hour teaching session on the topic of **"Should Christians Work?"** This is a very controversial topic here, but the Bible is very clear about it. I will not be allowed to finish this teaching because they have rejected it completely. Tonight we went out to another one of the cell groups. It was a very exciting meeting. Back on the last trip here, we had prayed for Prema's sister who was dying of cancer. The hospital gave her no hope of recovery. Well, here she is nearly two years later, completely healed and all the scans at the Mysore Hospital confirmed all the cancer has disappeared. Also the two Hindu men playing drums and an accordian have since been saved. Another woman was completely healed of a severe infection in her foot and leg. She was jumping with such joy and excitement. It was good once again to fellowship and to pray with these precious believers whom I first met 6 years ago. We came back home, had a big supper, and went to bed.

Tuesday, Feb. 13th-

It's a little cool and cloudy this morning, but that won't stop us from another good day of fellowship/ministry. After breakfast, we went to the 3 acre land he was given. We met there with a man who finds water among all the local farmers. He has never been wrong. He found where to bore the well and said it would produce an endless supply of water. He said the depth should be 330 feet. We've also been working on the design of the new buildings to be constructed. Early evening we went to two cell groups, including one new one. The first was a very quiet and gentle manifestation of the Holy Spirit, and the second was one of great joy as we met with one of the women I baptized in the river last year. We made a video last year of that day. We got home late, had supper and went to bed.

Wednesday, Feb. 14th-

We are very blessed again with a bright and sunny morning. Today I learned we will be going to Bangalore after Sunday service. But in the meantime, there are 6 more village cell groups to visit so we will have plenty to do. Right after breakfast, a young boy who was possessed by a demon, was brought to us by his parents. After only a short time, the demon left him and now he is well again. I've also been drawing some building plans for the first building. Today I finished it and it will be given to a local builder for a cost estimate. Also, I spent a few hours teaching Sharad and his workers about motivational gifts and spiritual manifestations. Before we knew it, it was already 1pm and time for lunch. Then more fellowship and a short time of rest before going out tonight to our cell group visitation about 25km from here. As always, the roads are absolutely horrible and it takes an hour to go such a short distance. This group is a new one and very well attended. Lots of prayer needs and we left from that place knowing our God had come in great power and much compassion. We came home rejoicing and had supper and good fellowship before bed time.

Thursday, Feb. 15th-

Once more, God has given us another beautiful, warm (88 F) sunny day. After breakfast, one of the local building contractors gave us his cost estimate for the 1st building, and we also gave the plans to a second contractor to compare prices. His cost was much better, his character was much more sincere, and we all liked his quiet, gentle spirit. He even asked us for prayer. I think we'll be using him. We spent some time at the land site doing our prayer walk and I drew up a sketch layout of the three buildings, coconut trees, banana trees, and sugar cane. We spent a lot of time there and we all became so excited about the land in how God has given it to the ministry. We came home for lunch and a little later, we went into the Nilgiri Mountains to see Vijaykumar but we missed him. I got some nice photos of wild monkeys and of some of the mountains. There will be no cell group tonight. We have only two more to visit - Friday night and Saturday night. Then Sunday morning service and then back to Bangalore.

Friday, February 16th-

It's 6:45am and my body has taken a full week to completely adjust to this time zone and I feel really excellent and refreshed. After breakfast, Sharad and Prema, Barnabas, George and Alphonsia, Munjo and myself went to the land and spent an hour or so there, just walking and praying, and believing God will provide everything needed to see "Camp Heaven" become a reality. Earlier, before breakfast, Sharad, Munjo and I walked to the river where I had baptized the gypsy boy 2 years ago. We also stopped at Pastor Danny's house for a quick visit. He wasn't home so we prayed with his wife and children and departed. Lunch was served around 1:30 and then a little rest before going out to this evening's cell group meeting. As I was praying along the way, I became very aware of a spirit who was strongly hindering or obstructing either the meeting or someone who wanted to come. After we were all assembled, a very familiar man came in. (I learned later his name is Ram, pronounced "Rahm"). He had grown a full beard since I saw him the last time. He was a totally shattered and broken man. His son had taken poison and committed suicide only 5 weeks ago. The son was not a believer, but the father is. He was the third person I baptized in the "elephant pond" 3 years ago. No one has been able to comfort him and he himself wanted to commit suicide over the grief of losing his son. So many of these believers just suffer quietly and tell no one. Many of the husbands are drunkards who beat their wives daily and abuse their children. This meeting was unlike the others in that all of us got "caught up" in the spirit together as the Lord ministered to this broken man and finally restored him. The Lord had a prophetic word for him saying that **"There are many children who have no father, and that the Lord would send many children to him to be a father figure to them".** Joy filled his heart as we hugged and all cried together with him. It was one of the most intense manifestations of God's compassion that I have witnessed in all 6 years of coming here. And then after we were finished praying for one another, the man went outside and brought me a baby lamb and put it in my lap. The lamb lay right down and was so at ease with such a stranger as myself. The ride home after was quiet as we were still in the spirit. It took a long time to "come back" like coming out of anesthesia at the hospital. We ate late and went to bed late, but with much joy and gladness at what the Lord had done.

Saturday, Feb. 17th-

Sadly, this is my last full day here with one final meeting tonight. I just don't know how the time can pass so quickly. Tomorrow (Sunday) we are leaving for Bangalore right after church is finished, but I know the Lord has a great day planned for us today. It's sunny and warm at 7am and 68 F. After breakfast, the Hindu man who received salvation brought his wife. She has wanted to be baptized for the past two years but she came too late last year so she waited until I came this year. So we went to the dam and did the baptism. On the way back, we stopped at the land and took photos of the new sign: "**Camp Heaven**" which had been put up while we were at the dam. It got very hot today reaching 96 degrees by 1:30pm while we were at the land. The couple came back and stayed with us for lunch and then prayer before they went back to their village. I won't see them again this year. Our last cell group meeting was at 7pm. Unlike the others, it was exceptionally dead, void of the Spirit; and very noticeably oppressive and heaviness. After the Word, when it was time to pray for the needs, some of the people got up and left. Just like my home church sometimes. I found out after the meeting, most of the people were Roman Catholic. So then I knew what was missing spiritually. No zeal, no joy, no excitement or gladness expressed during praise and worship; just staring straight ahead, showing no emotion at all. We went inside for tea afterwards and the whole room was filled with pictures of the Pope and Mary, one in which she was wearing a huge golden crown and lifted up above all. It was one of the most idolatrous and blasphemous attacks against the cross of Christ that I've ever witnessed, except in the Hindu temples around here. It is no wonder they were not interested in singing praise songs about Jesus. Needless to say, we were very sad for them to be under such bondage and control. We had supper and went to bed around 10:15pm.

Sunday, Feb. 18th-

Today began as another warm and sunny morning. We'll be having praise and worship and just communion service today and then prayer for the people. I think there is one more person who wants to be baptized after church, and if so, then after that, we will leave for Bangalore. The lady who wanted baptism didn't come, so after we prayed for all the people and said our goodbyes, we left at 12:30 for the long 6 ½ hour ride back to Bangalore. It doesn't take quite so long now because there is a new road for part of the way. We stopped twice for lunch and tea and got back at 7pm. I had time to send home an e-mail before Faith went to church. When it was 7pm here, it was 8:30am in Vermont. We had fellowship and supper and I went to bed at 10pm.

Monday, Feb. 19th-

I awakened to a sunny, humid morning here in Bangalore. I already miss the nice clean fresh mountain air of Talavadi. Sharad and I are going into the city for more rupees and just spend some time together. We rode in the car hired to take Hannah to school and kept it for a few hours. After going to the money exchange, we went to KFC and had our favorite: Thai veggie sticks. So needless to say, a very light lunch after coming home. We all just fellowshipped the rest of the afternoon and then Grace and I walked into the city to a nice coffee shop where we had a very flavorful cup of international Columbian coffee and it was absolutely delicious!! We all had supper around 9pm and I went to bed at 10:45pm.

Tuesday, Feb. 20th-

Bangalore greets us with another warm, sunny morning. Sharad and I were both up at 6:30am so we had a nice long walk before the traffic got to risky to walk in. After breakfast, we again rode with Hannah to school and then we went to a Café Coffee Day shop where I treated Sharad to the Columbian coffee and a very rich, tasty chocolate cake with frosting and walnuts. We enjoyed our time together then came back for lunch. Later at 6pm we're all going out to dinner to celebrate his 34th wedding anniversary. This will also be my last night in India for this trip. They all wanted to go to KFC so we went there. Then we came by the same Café Coffee Day shop and bought a whole cake like this morning's and brought it home to celebrate together and took photos. I then off to bed on a very full and stretched out belly. I know I have commented many times about going to bed with a very full belly. Eating a large meal late at night every night is the one thing that's very difficult to adjust to. If I don't eat a lot, Prema is offended and thinks I did not like her cooking. So what is a man like me to do? Just eat and be thankful!!

Wednesday, Feb. 21st-

It's warm and sunny at 6:45 already. Just like yesterday. Sharad is not up yet so I don't know if we'll take a walk or not. It's my last day here and we don't have any plans that I know of. Sometime during the afternoon, I'll probably have a hot bath and try to sleep a couple of hours. We'll be leaving at 11pm for the airport. We decided to go into town one more time for coffee and cake like yesterday. Then we home for lunch. I tried to sleep, but could not, so I got up after an hour and refreshed myself with a hot bath. We spent the rest of the evening fellowshipping and prayer time, then we supper at 9pm. I didn't eat much because I know there'll be two meals served on the flight back to Frankfurt. We left at 10:20pm for the one hour ride to the airport. It took about an hour to get to the boarding area, but now I'm in and I've got a couple hours before boarding time. My flight as always in the past journeys, was very timely to Frankfurt, Germany. The flight back to America was also timely and rather uneventful. Simon was waiting at JFK and we stopped for lunch on the way back to Vermont. I got home at 5pm.

Chapter Twelve
2008

Sunday, Mar. 3, 2008-

The Lord has very graciously opened a door of opportunity to go to Dipolog City in the southern island of Mindanao, Philippines with Bill and Ghing and Simon. Another brother in Christ (Thomas) from CT will go with us. We will fly from Hartford, CT on this Friday non-stop to LA., then to Guam, on to Manila, and finally to Dipolog City. This trip will be different for me. It has been many years (1998) since I went with others and much of this trip will concern and involve the medical humanitarian aid/supplies Renewed Life in Jesus sends to Dipolog City and its Provincial Hospital. I was invited mainly for two reasons. The first is to establish a church covering and credibility for Bill as our Philippines Missions Director, and the second reason is to dedicate a new church in honor of Bill's late wife Jane. Since I do not have a "God call" into the medical profession, I will be separate at times from the others, working with several local pastors; going to remote mountain villages with the Gospel and pray for the sick. This trip will be for three weeks and it has been planned since last August 2007. And the Lord has made full provision again this time.

Friday, Mar. 7th-

At 9:30am, Simon and Patty Jo picked me up. We drove to Don and Karen's. From there we all met for travel. Bill called that his van broke down in Brattleboro. So Simon and Patty Jo rode with Karen and I rode with Don. We transferred all the boxes to Don's truck and the luggage went into the van. AAA took Bill's van to Claremont and we left for Bradley. We all met there about 11:30 and got everything checked in, went through security and had lunch. We also met Thomas at the airport and we had a nice time of prayer before the five of us boarded our 6 hour flight to LA. What a beautiful flight. It was clear and sunny from the Great Lakes all the way to LA. We saw the spectacular Rocky Mountains and the Grand Canyon very clearly as we flew over them. We arrived at Lax right on time and changed terminals to Philippine Airlines. That flight left at 9:03pm CA time. It was a 12 hour non-stop flight to Guam where we landed for one hour to refuel. We flew all night in the dark over the Pacific Ocean, crossing the International Date Line where the twenty four time zones begin and end, so actually, we gained a whole day and I don't even know or understand what happened to Saturday!! All I know is we left on Friday and now it's Sunday. We did all get a pretty good amount of sleep on the plane. While refueling, we remained onboard the aircraft. We took off and flew for three more hours before arriving on

Sunday, Mar. 8th-

in Manila at 5:15am. We all had to retrieve our luggage, go through customs and immigration and recheck all baggage at the domestic flight terminal. We met and joined with one of Ghing's friends, Francesca from Manila. She will be flying with us to Dipolog City and spending the entire three weeks, staying at Ghing's mom's house We had a four hour layover and finally left on the 1 ½ hour flight south to Dipolog City. This flight was particularly beautiful, crossing several smaller islands along the way. There were many high mountains right near the coastline. When we arrived at the airport, we were offered an umbrella to protect us from the hot sunshine as we walked from the plane to the terminal. The weather is fantastic for me at 87F. It is very tropical, humid, and a bit toasty, just the way I like it. A large group of Bill's associates from the Provincial Hospital and Ghing's family and friends met us at the airport and helped us with all the boxes and luggage. We all got a very nice hotel room and then went for lunch. In all the years I've gone on short term missions trips, this was surely a first with a hotel room with air conditioning and a private bathroom with a shower. Simon, Bill and Ghing, went to visit the hospital and to make plans for their time here. I stayed at the hotel and attended the church service which meets on the top floor with Pastor Reyne. I will be with him most of the time. I spoke during the service today and Reyne has planned a busy schedule for my time here. We will all meet later for supper at Ghing's mom's house and then a good night's sleep will soon follow; yippee!!

Monday, Mar. 10th-

I slept well and woke up at 4:30am. I think it was because of the new time zone we are in. It is twelve hours ahead of Vermont time. Bill, Ghing, Simon and I went for a walk on the boardwalk at the beach. It's only two blocks from our hotel. It was still dark and I could see the lights on fishing boats just a mile or so off shore. It's very warm and humid, but nice. I'm teaming up today with Pastor Reyne and we are driving two hours away to dedicate a Christian Dental Service Ministry with Dr. Marvi (dentist). We will leave from the hotel at 8am after breakfast. So my first new day here has begun. We all so much enjoyed the excellent buffet breakfast, including rice, sardines with chili peppers, fresh fruit, (mango, pineapple, watermelon), and scrambled eggs. Bill, Ghing, Thomas, and Dr. Solano were picked up by a vehicle from the Provincial Hospital, taking them to spend the day working in the hospital. Pastor Reyne and I rode in the back of a small canvas-covered truck taking us to Liloy 2 ½ hours away, where we would meet up with Dr. Marvi. Pastor Philip drove the truck and he was no slow driver!! Along the way, I noticed how much it looked like India. I saw many of the same kinds of plants and trees, flowers, and landscape, except here it was a beautiful seaside. The waters are bluish green. We went to the dental outreach met with Dr. Marvi. She introduced me to her staff, allowed me to observe as she and the others cared for young children's dental problems, including pulling teeth as needed. We had a brief time of prayer as we dedicated her service to the Lord on behalf of the children who could not afford any dental care. She then arranged for us to travel by armed vehicle to the mayor's office to meet him. He then invited Pastor Reyne, Phillip, Dr. Marvi, and me for lunch at his sister's resort right directly on the waterfront. He also had well-armed men in uniforms all around us while we were on the property. We were served a wonderful assortment of food including raw fish in vinegar with green and red chili peppers, swordfish, rice, and fruit. Then we went back to the dental clinic where Dr. Marvi and her staff treated another large group of children during the afternoon. Then Reyne, Phillip, and I left for the 2 ½ hour ride back to Dipolog City. We got back around 5pm and went directly to another church where we had the opportunity to feed a gathering of homeless hungry children. Each of the children got only one small cup of juice, and one small roll, but at least it was something. That didn't do much for my broken heart to see these kids like this and to know how well our children at home are cared for. We all met back at the home of Ghing's mom for supper, checked and sent e-mails and walked back to our hotel. We went to bed at 9pm, after a long busy day.

Tuesday, Mar. 11th-

I woke up at 3:30am again, so I had some quiet time for reading and prayer. At 5:30 we all walked until 6am on the boardwalk. Then showered and had breakfast. Bill, Ghing, and Simon went to the hospital until lunchtime, and I went to Ghing's mom's house. I had some free time until 2pm, so I had plenty of time to do e-mails and talked with Faith on IM on the computer. At 2pm, Bill, Ghing, and I took a box of medical supplies to the mayor and she directed us to which clinic to bring them. At 4pm I went with Pastor Reyne on the motorbike to another feeding station for the children. The two of us had supper at the hotel restaurant. At 7pm, I was the speaker at a Full Gospel Businessmen's Meeting. I had a wonderful time of prayer for the men, and went back to my hotel room for the night. I was in bed again by 9:15pm.

Wednesday, Mar.12th-

I was awake and up at 3:30am again today. The same as yesterday, including our 5:30 walk. After we had breakfast, I was to be picked up at 8:15 to go to a local high school to speak at an assembly of the students. Well, we got there and discovered that the meeting had been cancelled. The school forgot to tell us they were giving final exams. So the students were not available. I then had a few hours of free time to go walk again by the sea and sit in the warm morning sunshine. Afternoon brought another cancellation because of scheduling conflicts, so we just all later enjoyed a wonderful evening dinner together. Ghing, Grace, and Francesca prepared Thai chicken curry and Dr. Malagos brought fresh crabs, clams, and rice. This was very delicious dinner, to say the least. All that food made us sleepy and so we were all in bed early.

Thursday, Mar. 13th-

We had our daily morning seaside walk at 5:30 and then breakfast. Dr. Solano and Ghing went to the hospital again to do surgery. Bill and I spent two hours in the hotel restaurant talking with an American man who was running away from his Philippine wife. After praying with him, we convinced him to go back home and reconcile. He didn't seem to want to and we don't know if he did. We didn't see him again.

Later in the afternoon, I went with Pastor Reyne and Phillip into a Muslim area in the slums to feed more hungry kids. Then I was invited to speak at small church in the early evening. After dark, we held our 1st outside crusade in a Muslim area. There was a flat bed truck in a field and it was used as a stage. A cloth screen was set up on the truck bed to show the Jesus film. The field soon filled with people, and spread into the roads around the field. There were armed police surrounding the field and protecting us the whole time. After I spoke, we had the altar call for salvation and over 100 people came to Christ. They had raised their hands so we could see and pray for them. Then we prayed for any who were sick. I was not allowed to go into the crowd to lay hands on anyone so I just prayed a public prayer for healing for those who said they were sick.

Friday, Mar. 14th-

This morning was warm and cloudy and we were up early for our walking time. After breakfast, I had an 8:30 evangelism/dental outreach meeting, held in a large warehouse. I was picked up by Phillip on his motorbike and on the way, it began to rain, so we parked the bike and went by pedicab. As like last night, a film of Jesus was shown, and then I spoke from the parable of **"The Pearl of Great Price".** Then I had an altar call. Again, like the night before, more than 100 people raised their hands for salvation and we prayed with them for that. After their salvation they were cared for by local Christian dentists for cleaning teeth, teachings on oral hygiene, etc. After lunch, I was the guest speaker at a very formal military graduation ceremony of a class of ROTC Naval Cadets. These men looked so sharp in their crispy bright white uniforms as they marched into the hall proudly waving the flag of the Philippines. Even with a full beard, I was very well received by these young cadet graduates and the military officers in attendance. I was invited for another lunch, this time with the college President and several top school officials. They were all very kind and gracious to me as we ate and fellowshipped around the table.

After supper, I was invited to speak at a youth rally of all teens and early 20's. They meet weekly in a back room of a local restaurant. After such a formal afternoon at the ROTC graduation, this meeting was so much fun with free spirit worship with a live band playing

Hillsong praise songs. I certainly had no trouble going to sleep later on.

Saturday, Mar. 15th-

This morning brought our same routine of walking on the boardwalk. This time, however, being the weekend, we went to the farmer's market where we could buy all sorts of fresh fruits, veggies, and fish. I had two barbecued bananas which tasted really good as an appetizer before eating breakfast. My only commitment today was late afternoon. Phillip picked me up on his motorbike and took me to a different feeding location for homeless hungry children about a half hour away by motorbike. Later on, I had time to do e-mail and IM from the computer at Ghing's mom's house. I ended my evening by attending the twelve year opening celebration of the fast food café in the hotel. I sat with the mayor, the owner, and all the employees. The mayor had previously asked me to come, and I considered myself very privileged to do so. There were many varieties of food and a very nice whole roasted pig. So once again I went to bed with a full belly. I'm so glad I get to "walk it off" each morning.

Sunday, Mar. 16th-

We enjoyed our early morning walk and breakfast. I'll be picked up by motorbike around 8:30am to speak at a church service where we fed children earlier this week. Bill, Ghing, and Simon came too and each of us had the opportunity to speak and after we were finished, the band played more praise and worship and invited me to play with them. It was a great morning. Then we had lunch at Ghing's mom's, then walked back to the hotel for a couple of hours before the next service on the fourth floor of this hotel, where I spoke last Sunday, right after we arrived. This time, it was nice to see some familiar faces. I taught on **"Holding fast our profession of faith"** and demonstrated with a rope. After the meeting, we went to supper at Dr. Malago's new house. She asked me to pray and bless the meal. We had a huge dinner including a whole roast pig. She also had many of her family and when the meal was finished, there was nothing left except the pig's head and bones. We stayed late and fellowshipped. It was the second night out of my whole time here that I had no meetings so it was nice to spend the evening with Bill, Ghing, Simon, Thomas, and some new friends here.

Monday, Mar. 17th-

My day began with our morning walk, breakfast, and then off with Phillip. He and I went to another feeding area for the homeless and hungry children. I had the rest of the day free. This evening, Bill and Ghing, Thomas, Simon, and I went to dinner at the home of a doctor friend of Dr.Malago. What a contrast for me to have just been with starving children this morning and now in this very rich environment, enjoying the lavish house, good food, fish, shellfish, and fruit. But there is a stark contrast in all nations between the poor and the rich. I thank God for the opportunity to dwell in peace with both. Then a very steady heavy rain set in for the whole night.

Tuesday Mar. 18th-

This morning began with steady rain still falling, so no walking today. After breakfast, the rain stopped. I was taken by motorbike by another pastor named Jonathan. He was younger than Phillip, but a very kind and gentle man with a wife and children. He took me into the jungle as far as we could go on the motorbike, then we walked for about 35 minutes more, crossing over the Dipolog River on a bamboo pole footbridge. We went to where you would never know people lived there in old, rundown, bamboo huts with dirt floors. We shared the Word of God with all of them, as there were so few, maybe 20 – 30 in the whole cluster of houses. Then Jonathan and I laid hands on each of them for various sicknesses, etc. I later found out that this was a very dangerous place to go. It is a hideout for Abu Sayef rebels. I didn't feel threatened in any way and the people seemed very happy we came to see them. Afterwards, I came back to Ghing's mom's house and had lunch with Bill, Ghing, and Simon. Then I walked back to the hotel, changed and walked for two hours at the sea wall. This evening we had another outside crusade planned, but it got rained out. It rained all night.

Thursday, Mar. 20th-

After our morning walk and breakfast, I was notified that there would be no meetings this morning so I had some free time again. Pastor Reyne took me to the home of an old man who has bone cancer and I prayed for him. I had all the rest of the day to myself, so I sent e-mails and IM with Faith. I rested much of the day, and after supper, we all went to the mayor's house for his weekly Bible study. It was quite lengthy and I got back to the hotel around 11pm.

Friday, Mar.21st-

Today is my spiritual birthday of 26 years as a believer. As we walked at the seaside, I had much to meditate on and to thank God for. Today, all of us have a day off for rest. We finally got to go to the beach and swim in the warm Sulu Sea. The sand is black but still very nice. The sun was very good too. Thomas didn't want to use any sun lotion and he got absolutely fried red with blisters soon to follow. Ghing's family brought a great picnic lunch which we really enjoyed. After, we all just did nothing the rest of the afternoon until around 4pm. Then we went to the hospital to visit some of Simon's patients and prayed for their speedy recovery. We had supper at the hotel tonight and went to bed early. Our day at the beach made us all very sleepy.

Saturday, Mar. 22nd-

Today began with another beautiful early morning walk. The full moon was just setting over the ocean, and the temperature was a comfortable 82 degrees. After breakfast, one more attempt will be made to go up the mountain where the new church is being built. There are about eighty believers who live on the upper part of the mountain and they have no church building to meet in. This is the church built in honor of Jane. I have been carrying a hand carved wooden plaque and Don sent with us a cross made entirely of wooden toothpicks. We will present these to the pastor of this new church. There has up to now, been no break from the rains in the higher mountains. The road up has been washed out and the construction vehicles have had great difficulty in completing the project. We are waiting for a current report on conditions at the site and we should know something by 9:30. The trip will be by mountain bikes if we can even go. Word has just come; the summit is clear, no rain, and the mountain road is useable. We used three city motorbikes (one bike and a driver for each of us: (Bill, Simon, and myself) to travel from Dipolog City, a distance which took about 45 minutes to the base of the mountain. Then we transferred to 3 very heavy duty mountain bikes for the 45 minute climb to the church site which is probably around 4500 feet up. Our pictures will show what a beautiful place this church is located in and how rough the trail is to get there. The building is not yet finished but we did leave the plaque and the cross and had the dedication service, and prayed for a few who were sick. By the time we got back from the mountain, it was mid-afternoon. We had a late lunch and fellowship.

Sunday, Mar. 23rd-

Our day began with the morning walk and breakfast. Bill and Ghing went to the Polanco church, and Simon went with me to another church where we both spoke. Later, I spoke at the 3pm service at the hotel on the fourth floor. That was my last scheduled speaking engagement.

Monday, Mar. 24th-

We all met with the Governor at 7:30am. This was a very formal, partially outside meeting where Simon and Bill were presented with certificates of appreciation for service to Dipolog and the hospital. Then he invited us into his dining room for coffee and snacks. Then Simon went back to do more surgeries. I went to pray for a young pastor's new business. At 4pm the Governor sent two of his personal government cars to pick us up to attend a large outdoor sports celebration where we were seated with all of his staff and officials on the platform with him. Even though he is the highest ranking political official, he was very cordial and kind toward us, and made us all feel welcome. Then we went to dinner with the Governor. We had our own table and three waitresses to attend to us. This was our last dinner before leaving this beautiful place. Now its 9pm and we are back in our hotel packing for our long trip home tomorrow.

Tuesday, Mar. 25th-

We had our final morning walk and breakfast. We are taking our luggage early to the airport and checking it through to Los Angeles. We'll still have a couple of hours before flight time so we'll go back to Ghing's mom's home for a while. Francesca will travel back to Manila with us, and she will remain there where she lives. Our plane leaves at 12:25pm for Manila. Everything went like clock work and we were inside and through security in no time. The flight from Dipolog to Manila was just as beautiful as the photos from the plane will show. The flight also offered me a special quiet time of meditation and reflection on why the Lord had given me this great privilege, and I will always be so very thankful. There was a bit of sadness as we got higher and higher and further away. I met some very precious beloveds in the faith while here and I was so thankful for such a very special trip this time. It was a true honor to be asked by Bill to dedicate the new church in honor of our beloved Jane who is now with the Lord, to have met Dr. Malagos and her staff at the Provincial Hospital, to see with my own eyes, the hospital beds some of us had loaded into cargo containers and shipped from America. There is some talk of "hooking up" with Springfield Hospital as a "sister" hospital and sending a team with Dr. Solano again to perform many more life-saving surgeries. It was also very gratifying to have met many of the Government officials with whom Bill has established professional relationships with to help watch over and secure the delivery of the medical supplies that have been donated and shipped here. Bill's own medical experience as an EMT has brought a wealth of value to such a needy community.

We arrived in Manila 25 minutes early. We had to go to the international terminal from the domestic terminal. We found a nice cafeteria and stayed there for a couple hours and finally it was time to leave Francesca. It was a teary moment, as she is such a close friend to Ghing. Now, we've all come through security again and are in our boarding area. We still have 4 ½ hours to wait, but we got here early and got some good seats to wait in. Finally, it was time for boarding and the twelve hour flight returning us to Los Angeles. (Thomas was still bleeding through the blisters of the sunburn, and we found a small medical shop in the airport to "patch him up"). We had a three hour layover before our early morning flight to Atlanta, which took another four hours. We had time for a quick breakfast together at the Atlanta airport and then our final two hour flight to Hartford, CT. Don was there to meet us and we all came home very tired, but spiritually fulfilled, as God once again presented us such a wonderful opportunity. And so another trip has come to an end. I don't really know if I will ever go to Dipolog City again, but I do know that all the while I was there, my heart was still in India, and it burns to go again (to India). But that will be entirely up to the Lord. I am very willing as long as He continues to provide for me to go; then I will go.

Chapter Thirteen
2009

Nov. 21st, 2008-

It has been in my heart for some time to bring another Board Member from Renewed Life. I believe it is important to have another come with me to witness the ministry in India which we support as a church, in the event that I may not always be able to go. The Lord has provided just such a man. He came to Renewed Life several years back and got saved there. He has a very evangelistic spirit and he seems to "fit" the criteria needed to make such a journey. Such a person cannot be fearful, squeamish, or a complainer about the food and sleeping accommodations. Tom set well with my spirit and I invited him to come along on this next wonderful and exciting trip to India.

We are not leaving until April 14th but it is important to release our faith early for the travel visas necessary, and good airfare rates, along with all the monetary provisions needed for such a journey.

Tom and I are greatly rejoicing today because our visas came back from the Indian Consulate and our plane tickets were purchased. This year British Airways has the best price, so we will be flying from JFK to London and then, non-stop to Bangalore. We have time enough in London to have a visit with our friends Jill and Ian, who live only 15 minutes from Heathrow Airport where we will land. We will leave from New York on Tuesday, April 14th at 6:15pm. I have also decided to make these trips to India in April from now on, so it will not leave Faith here in Vermont having to deal with heavy, late-winter snow-storms on her own.

Apr. 3rd, 2009-

It has been wonderful watching our faithful God as He has so abundantly provided for this trip. Tom and I are very excited with only 11 days before we leave. Ministry plans have been made in India and new mattresses purchased because the rats have eaten the old ones. Much funding has come in and I'll be getting my traveler's checks on Monday.

Tom's daughter, Samantha, is driving us to JFK and Jeremiah and Felicia will pick us up. Ken and Don will cover the two Sunday services at Renewed Life and Phil will cover the Bible studies. There are many strong believers who will be faithful to pray for one another and to minister to one another as needed.

Monday, Apr. 13th-

6:20pm – I received an e-mail from British Airways informing me that I could now check us both in online and print our boarding passes good all the way to India. Tom and I exchanged e-mails with Ian and Jill to make the final arrangements for a short visit with them while we will be in London.

Tuesday, April 14th-

7:20am – It is26F and frosty. I'll be leaving home in an hour. Faith is driving me to Friendly's in Brattleboro to meet Tom and Samantha. From there the three of us head for JFK. We should arrive by 2pm.

Our trip to JFK was fast - only 3½ hours. So we arrived at 12:30 and were in and through security in less than 10 minutes. We walked around a lot, had lunch, and walked some more. This was good exercise since we will be sitting for a long time on the flight. Finally, our boarding call was announced about 5:40pm. Our seats were very good, a nice smooth flight with an excellent dinner served over St. John's Island- New- found-land, followed by a few hours of much needed sleep. High altitude sunrise greeted us over western Ireland, while below us the land was still quite dark.

.Wednesday, Apr. 15th-

After a seven hour flight, we landed at Heathrow Airport in London around 6:30am London time. We had the pleasure of coming into British Airways brand new famous Terminal 5. Ian and Jill were waiting for us; so we left the airport and spent 2 ½ hours at their flat. We enjoyed a wonderful visit and good tea and goodies. It was great to get out of the "airport scene" for a couple of hours Now we're back at the airport, we've gone through security, had lunch and are waiting in the boarding gate area for our 9 ½ hour flight to Bangalore. We leave at 1:40pm London time, so that's only another hour and 10 minutes. We fully expect our flight to be as excellent as the first one.

It was cloudy and light rain when we arrived, but now it is sunny and near 70F. India will be much hotter with temps around 105F the day we arrive. (Tomorrow morning)

Thursday, Apr. 16th-

We arrived in Bangalore at 3:20am - 20 minutes early. It was another beautiful flight as we traveled southeast across Germany, Austria, Greece, western Turkey, Saudi Arabia, then across the Arabian Sea, finally crossing the India coast just south of Goa, a very famous tourist resort on the seaside. The new airport was super and we were through immigration, baggage and customs in only 15 minutes. Sharad, Prema, and Dominic were waiting for us. What a wonderful reunion and a one hour drive back to Sharad's flat, followed with much good fellowship. Due to a lack of sleeping accommodations, Tom is staying downstairs with Dominic (Sharad's son-in-law) and his family and I am upstairs with Sharad and his family. Tom went to bed around 8:30am and I went around 10am, and I slept until 12:30 midday. We had a cool water shower, lunch, and then we went into the city to cash some of our traveler's checks. We all stayed up visiting until 10pm. After Prema's chicken curry, we slept very well.

Friday, Apr. 17th-

I got up at 6:30 and found it to be a very warm and sunny morning. Tom and Dominic came upstairs to Sharad's flat for breakfast and a short time of fellowship. We then went into the city for supplies we would need for our ministry time in Talavadi. We had Lunch at KFC, and I enjoyed introducing Tom to one of my favorite fast-food snacks; Thai veggie sticks. He liked them very much! We'll be spending the night here and leave around 6am for the 7 hour drive. It will be nice to go to the mountains; it's been quite warm here in Bangalore at 105F both yesterday and today. I think Tom is a bit shocked by these temperatures, but he'll adjust.

Saturday, Apr. 18th-

I awoke at 4am with the excitement of finally finishing the long journey from America to Talavadi, South India. I got up early to finish packing, and soon the others in the family were up also. Some will go with us, others will stay back. It was a wonderful prayerful send off and at 6:10am we were on our way. We got out of Bangalore before the traffic got heavy on this sunny, clear morning with some early morning haze in the air. Hannah got car sick about an hour into the trip, so we stopped for a few minutes for her to freshen up a bit. Then we prayed with her and continued on (stopping after three hours of travel) in Mysore for breakfast. Then we continued on for another 3 ½ hours of travel, finally reaching our "base camp" about 1:30pm. There were many people waiting to greet us with flowers and hugs and some tears of joy. Tom was greeted in the same manner by brethren he had never known before. It has been two years since I was last here. (Last year, I was in the Philippines). We then had lunch, fresh, cool water shower, and then a short restful nap. Then we went to the land "Camp Heaven". It was such a great time of prayer and walking on the land. By now, Tom was really "into" this trip and his first. We had a late supper and went to bed a little early tonight (9:30). Tom and I will both speak during the morning church service (10am).

Sunday, Apr. 19th-

All of us were awakened at 5am by the Muslim call to prayer, so there will be no more sleeping this morning, as loud speakers on the tower of the mosque carried the sounds. But that is normal here, even though it is so invasive and forced upon every person in the village. After breakfast, the children had their "kid's church". It was so wonderful to see so many and hear them singing so lovely.

Then the adults came for the 10am service. Many came by bus or walked. Some wanted prayer even before the service started. It was very special for me to see so many of the people I've known since first coming in 2001. Tom and I both spoke; then we prayed for all the people. Not one of them left until they were all prayed for. It was 2pm by the time we had lunch. We will be going out to a nearby village at 5pm to minister to the people. I can tell that Tom is already deeply touched as he witnesses the power of the Holy Spirit outpouring of mercy, compassion, and healing among the people. When we arrived at a certain house for the meeting, it was filled with children and some elderly people, several whom I've known from previous years. It was such a joy to see so many kids so eager to sing and learn about Jesus. This house was a new cell group started by George. I taught them Proverbs 3:5. It took repeating the verse only three times for them to learn it. Then prayer time came and once again, every single person in the house wanted prayer, from the youngest to the oldest. The kids all wanted prayer for these things:

1. They would be healthy
2. They would get a good education
3. They would get a good job
4. Their houses would be filled with peace.

Most of the adults were concerned with health issues including failing eyesight, aches and pains. The Holy Spirit was very gracious and gentle to them all, relieving them of their infirmities. After prayer, we had a nice time of fellowship, a slow, bumpy ride back to Talavadi and the normal late- evening supper.

Monday, Apr. 20th-

Today and all this week, I will be teaching the Bible school class on the subject of **"Our Words".** After breakfast, we started about 9am. I did two sessions of 45 minutes with a short tea break in between. This class of 8 students is very hungry for the Word and some have come from far away. There are two married couples in the class (one with a young child). Pastor Sharad interpreted the first session and another pastor in the class interpreted the second session. Later in the afternoon, we went to a nearby village just to pray for two men. Then we went on to another village to visit the girl God healed from boils all over her body. She wasn't home, so we prayed with her mom and a few others in the house. Then we went to see a woman who is now 98 years old. When the girl was healed from the boils, that lady used to walk to every meeting I had for six years in a row. It was a very happy reunion time to see each other again. There were many others gathered at her house who came to see us and for prayer. We stayed after for tea and got a late start home. Along the way, the gas pedal cable broke and our driver had to drive by pulling the cable with one hand. He could not use the gas pedal. It was quite difficult because the roads are so horrible. The cable kept slipping out of his hand. But we finally got home around 10:40pm. Supper was late, but tasty then off to bed.

Tuesday, Apr. 21st-

We've been here a week from home already and the days are hot; 98F to 105F even here in the mountainous villages at 6000 feet elevation above sea level. The nights are cool and comfortable. There have been some scattered late afternoon thunderstorms around.

Today, I'll continue the class. I taught two sessions in the morning; then we broke for lunch. Tom and Sharad worked on filming for the ministry and I taught another session until 4:35pm. I finished the study on "words" after 6½ hours of class time. We had tea and cookies then went to a village some 25km away. It took quite a while to get there because of the bad roads. There was a very strong spirit of oppression upon the people. So strong you could actually feel it. Most of the people had been believers a year ago, but have returned to Hinduism. They were told they would be given ten acres of land for each family if they would renounce Christ. One lady refused and got no land. Tom spoke at this meeting, and then we prayed for the people, including a young man who got his right hand chopped completely off at the wrist from an accident in the place he worked. There was another man who was carried in by the others. He could not walk and could not talk. We do expect to hear of good reports coming in over the next couple of days. That's how we find out the good things God has done. It was late when we got home.

Wednesday, Apr. 22nd-

It rained hard in the night but it is nice and warm 80F. I love it!!! Tom and I had the morning to just play with all the street kids. They love the attention. I taught the afternoon session on the **"Sower and the Seed"** then later we went out to another village. It was just the opposite from the night before: much joy and rejoicing and celebrating. Nearly all the people remembered me from every trip before, going back to 2001. we had a great time of prayer as God poured out the rain of His Holy Spirit. We had heavy rain and thunderstorms outside and the power went out, so we just carried on with our flashlights. Then we had candlelight tea and fellowship. We arrived home earlier tonight because the village was close by.

Thursday, Apr. 23rd-

We had rain most of the night. We were scheduled to go high into the Nilgiri Mountains to some tribal village but the rain has been much worse in the mountains so the meeting has been delayed. It will take us five hours one way if we get to go there at all. The rainy season has started and now some of the roads are washing out. I had hoped coming in mid April that it would still be hot and dry. So I don't know yet where we might go instead. It's getting dark in my room. The power goes out early morning from 8-10am and again from 4-5pm. Tom and I had all day to fellowship and share all the great things God has done this week. Pastor Sharad finished the Bible school last class this afternoon. Then we left for a village 27km from here. It took 1 ½ hours to go only 18 U.S. miles because the roads are so bad. We went through what is called "the forest" which I've been through every year. Many of the local people are fearful because of the wild elephants which have attacked and overturned vehicles at times. I've been through that forest 14 times and have never seen an elephant. I have seen some monkeys and a couple of wild boars. Those would make a very tasty dinner. The house we went to filled up quickly. We started the meeting outside with George's ministry to the children. They all sat down in the street, some sitting in cow dung. It was good to see so many kids singing loudly praising Jesus in public. All the people in the other houses came out to see what was going on. We prayed for five sick kids and that started a huge throng of people coming from the whole village for prayer. It took Tom and I nearly 45 minutes to pray for the ones who were already in the house. It seemed to us that the people just kept coming from everywhere. We moved into one room of the house and it filled in no time, then the second room filled, and the whole outside of the house and into the street filled up with people of all ages. Tom spoke tonight and then we began to pray for all the new people we hadn't yet prayed for. They all, every single one of them, wanted prayer for all sorts of sickness and family problems. Tom took one room and I took the other room. It took nearly an hour and then we went outside to the street and prayed with many more. Then we were taken to another house to pray for a young woman and her two children. They were too sick and weak to come to the meeting. We found them lying on the floor under mosquito netting. By the time everyone had been prayed for, we had been there 3 ½ hours instead of the usual 1 ½ hours. We were so blessed to experience such a glorious outpouring of God's mercy and compassion. Tom could hardly speak all the way home. We never see this kind of thing at home. We got back around 10pm and got word that we cannot go to the tribal village in the high mountains. The road is gone due to a week of very heavy rain there. Also, I got a wedding invitation from Ram,(the man whose youngest son had committed suicide when I was here two years back). It is the same man who gave me the little lamb. The wedding is at 10:30am on Sunday so Prema will take me, along with Tom. Then we'll come back here for our Sunday service and Dominic's children's program. So it looks like Sunday will be a full day.

Friday, Apr. 24th-

It is clear and cooler this morning at 72F. I woke up early, still thinking about and rejoicing over last night's meeting. I don't know what we'll be doing today yet, but I know we'll be going to another village later this afternoon or early evening. I taught in the Bible school for two hours today and played kick ball with some of the street kids and had lots of fun. I beat them badly, then we had tea and left for ministry in a village about one hour away. That meeting was another very exciting one, being with so many people I've known for 8 years. Many testified of being healed the last time I was here. Much joy and celebration in the house and then a great time of ministry followed. Tom has adjusted very nicely and is of much help praying with the people. They all quickly received him in every meeting. His height is the topic of much conversation as he towers over the very short Indian people. Tonight is our last village meeting already, but many will come for Sunday service. Another late supper soon followed by sweet peaceful sleep.

Saturday, Apr. 25th-

It rained last night and now it is cloudy and cool - 75 degrees. Today after breakfast we went to the land (Camp Heaven) and laid out where the church will be built. That was a very exciting time. Then we came back to the house, had lunch, and a very big meeting. The mountain people came here, along with two other pastors, the Bible school students, and some people from one of the other villages where we had visited during the week. A very good meeting and once again, every person wanted prayer. That meeting lasted until nearly 5:30pm. Then we had coffee and returned to the land so I could lay the cornerstone of the foundation, and by faith see the building completed. We also had enough extra money given this year to pay for half of the fencing around the property. That construction will take place after we have returned to the U.S. next week.

While I was at the land, the "vomit comet" hit me suddenly with no warning. I have never been sick on any other trip since starting in

1991. I got poisoned by some spoiled milk in the coffee and had neglected to pray before I drank it - that won't happen again.

Sunday, Apr. 26th-

We received more heavy rain in the night. I feel very excellent and ready for a good breakfast. A busy day follows with the wedding at 10:30 in another village, then back here for the church meeting, then a special children's program. Just while we were eating breakfast John Wesley (the father of the young girl healed of boils all over her body in 2001) came in. He just won a large court settlement for $80,000 and now wants to pay cash for the new Bible school at Camp Heaven, finish the new electric pump for the well, and get the electricity connected. What a blessing to wake up to. So we went quickly to the land to show him where the school would be built. Then we hurried to the wedding which was such a joyous celebration. Then back here to pray for all the people who came. Many were in the road outside because they could not go into the house. Then the Sunday school children performed several skits and dances which we now have on video. We enjoyed lunch, a short rest, then off again to VJ Kumar's house for a new cell group meeting. A very small in number had gathered, but Holy Spirit was very strong. Now we have had supper and are packing for our 5am ride back to Bangalore. Our ministry mission for Talavadi has come to an end and we are a little sad it finished so quickly, but knowing we will be home with our families in the USA in four more days is a very nice thought.

Monday, Apr. 27th-

It was cool and still dark as we left Talavadi at 5:10am. There was no traffic, and excellent driving conditions. We stopped for buffet breakfast at a very nice hotel restaurant in Mysore, then on to Bangalore arriving at 11:30am. We made excellent time because part of the road is new since I was last here. It is very warm at 107F. I had my first hot shower in 2 weeks, sent e-mails home, called home, had lunch and just rested the rest of the afternoon. Dominic invited me to speak at a pastor's seminar tomorrow morning at 11am. After that, Tom and I exchanged the rest of our traveler's checks and did some gift shopping. We had a big homecoming dinner tonight and all the daughters prepared the meal. I can hardly take a deep breath now. Well off to bed - it's 10:15pm

Tuesday, Apr. 28th-

A very warm 84F at 6am to enjoy coffee outside. Very nice; I checked our flight status with British Airways and all looks good. Tomorrow morning I can print our boarding passes. We have only one hour and five minutes in London to make the connection to NYC but that should be plenty of time. I had the blessing of ministering at a pastor's seminar from 11am till noon. Tom, Grace, Hannah, Sharad and I went into the city to do some gift shopping and while we were in a card shop in the middle of Bangalore, we met John M's daughter from my home town of Chester. He told us she would be coming but we didn't really think we would ever see her in a city of 11,000,000 people.

We came back to Sharad's flat, had lunch and fellowship and Tom worked on Sharad's computer and printer to do some very necessary repairs. A late evening supper, then off to bed (our last night here).

Wednesday, Apr. 29th-

Another delightfully warm morning greeted us at 84F. There is something special to me about how much I love getting up to warm mornings. I checked in online for our flights and printed the boarding passes. All looks good for our departure to the airport at 2am. In the meantime, Tom is with Sharad buying some Bibles for new believers and I am going in a little while for my traditional visit with Grace to an international coffee house. We will all go out together as a family later for dinner, then a short time of fellowship and prayer, and "try" to sleep before leaving the house at 2am (sleep before such a trip is usually just a word). It's usually too much excitement about coming back home to be thinking about sleeping.

Thursday, Apr. 30th-

2am - Wow!! I did it. I actually slept soundly. We had a very nice dinner then a time of prayer and I was in bed at 9:40pm. I slept right up to 1:45am. I jumped up quickly and even had time for tea because all things were already packed. We left for the airport at 2am, arriving at 2:45 and it was clear, calm, and warm 84 degrees. What a blessing this new airport is; so spacious, modern, comfy with AC. Shops, café, nice chairs, everything so smooth and efficient compared to the old military airport. It only took us both 10 minutes for bag check in, customs and immigration and security and we were in the boarding gate area. We even have 2½ more hours to spare. There were no lines, we had lots of time to sit in the café, and now we are sitting in a very comfy airport chair. Once on board the aircraft, we even got the bulkhead seats on the flight to London, sitting directly behind business class and loads of leg room. The flight left right on time and we actually got into London 20 minutes early. There was another plane at the gate so we had to wait for it to depart before we could park and de-plane. We didn't get much sleep because of five screaming and crying kids sitting right near us, but we survived very nicely. We had a very close connection in London and made our flight to JFK with only six minutes to spare! (That certainly is a little too close for an international flight for my liking!) We got into JFK five minutes late, but not bad, and straight through immigration and customs, baggage claim and out of the airport in less than 10 minutes. Jeremiah and Felicia were waiting for us and the four of us had a very nice time of fellowship and ride back to Vermont with a food stop in Connecticut. We dropped Tom off in Brattleboro where Carol was waiting for our arrival at 9:15pm. I got home just before 10pm, showered and stayed up until close to midnight before going to bed. I slept very well and woke up refreshed and ready at 5:45am for my first day home. Praise the Lord for His wonderful care and provision again this trip.

Chapter Fourteen
April 2010

Friday, Apr. 9, 2010

(Faith's birthday today) and these trips continue into another year. Once again, God has provided for Tom and I to return to beloved India. We will depart this year from Logan airport in Boston, stopping at Heathrow in London. We will have time there for a short visit with Ian and Jill,(but not leaving the airport this time), before we leave on the very long 10 hour flight to Bangalore. We will still have this weekend to spend with our families and loved ones, before we actually depart at 9:30pm on Tuesday April 13th.

Tuesday, Apr. 13, 2010-

I left our house at 1:45pm and drove to Keene to meet Tom. I left my truck there and rode with him to Manchester, NH where we left his truck and took a shuttle bus to Logan Airport in Boston. It was a very nice ride even in all the traffic, as we shared in the excitement of our second trip together. We arrived at our terminal at 6pm and at 6:08pm we were already through bag check-in and security and ordering our supper in a very nice restaurant. We are now in our boarding area and our flight to London will leave in only two more hours.

Wednesday, Apr. 14th-

Heathrow Airport, London- We arrived a few minutes late but an excellent flight. Ian and Jill met us downstairs and we had nearly an hour and a half of great fellowship, tea, and muffins. At 11am we came back through security; (very fast, no lines). Now we're waiting in the boarding area for our 2:10pm flight for India.

Again, it was another wonderful flight to Bangalore. 9 ½ hours, 2 very good meals on the plane and we got some sleep as well.

Thursday, Apr. 15^{th-}

At 4:30am India time, we touched down smoothly on the runway. It only took one hour to process through immigration, customs and baggage claim so we were out of the airport by 5:30am. Sharad, Prema, and Grace were waiting just outside. What a joy to see their happy, smiling faces after thirty hours of travelling. It was another hour in the van and we arrived at Sharad's flat around 6:30am. We had a great time of sharing and fellowship, we checked for e-mails, and slept for a short time (one hour for me, four hours for Tom). After lunch, we went into town to exchange travel checks into rupees. We spent the rest of the day just resting and fellowship. I went to bed at 9:15pm and slept until 7:30am Friday morning.

Friday, Apr. 16th-

There were no vans available to rent to go to Talavadi so we just stayed and rested and fellowshipped. A van became available for Saturday, so we all went to bed early and got up at 4am.

Saturday Apr. 17th-

It's now 4am. I had time to check and send e-mail, had tea and fruit for breakfast, then we loaded the van and at 5am we were on our way for the long, hot, dusty, bumpy ride to Talavadi (6 ½ hours this year due to some new road paving). As soon as we arrived, some people came to the house for prayer. We had a big thunderstorm and my room got flooded from a leaky roof, but we can fix that tomorrow. We went 8km to a cell group meeting, and as always, every person wanted prayer. We know there will be testimonies coming. The power also went out in the storm, but it is back on now. I had a light supper, and am now writing in this journal. It's nearly 10pm and tomorrow, we will have ministering opportunities during the Sunday service.

Sunday, Apr. 18th-

It's 6:30am and I slept very well and I'm looking forward to what the Lord will do today. It's clear and cool at about 82 degrees F. Service began at 10am. The power had already gone out at 9am, so it got hot fast with a small room full of people and no fans. But as always, the Lord was very much present, answering so many needs, but one in particular: one little girl only fours years old asking God to stop her father from drinking and to return him to their home and family. That was a very tender moment in a room filled with other children and adults. We had a late lunch and some rest time. A very violent thunderstorm came and the power went out again for awhile. In the evening, we had a very good meeting with all the staff of Honey-comb Ministries discussing current ministry growth and new needs. I went to bed late and was awakened by another heavy thunderstorm and the roof leaking very badly on my bed, so I just got up and moved the mat to another place in the house and went back to sleep. No big deal.

Monday, Apr. 19th-

We all awakened to find much storm damage. We drove to a nearby village to check and write e-mails. We stopped at Camp Heaven for a prayer walk on the land. There had been a plan to go to the gypsy camp in the late afternoon but then we found out their village and roads were washed out and their homes were flooded, so we could not go. We stayed home and fellowshipped and enjoyed our evening together discussing ministry needs with George.

Tuesday, Apr. 20th-

It is another warm, sunny morning. I had the joy of teaching the ten Bible School students today and found out none of them were saved yet, so I taught them about being born again. At the end of the class, all ten students and our driver got saved. It was very powerful to see the immediate change in every one of them. We had lunch and rested awhile before going to the forest village one hour away. This village is where eight years ago, the boy who was born crippled and could not walk, got healed. I saw him again and now he is 18 years old and he is the shepherd of his father's flock of sheep. We were very happy to see each other again. The house meeting was very full to where there was no more room for anyone else. Tom shared the Word and then we prayed for all the people as we always do. We stayed for tea made with fresh milk and it was so good. Then an hour-long ride home, supper and fellowship, and just celebrating the goodness of the Lord today and the eleven new souls in God's Kingdom. I am now very ready for a good sleep at 10:30.

Wednesday, Apr. 21st-

A new plan and a surprise for us: we will be leaving Talavadi on this Saturday at 4:30am because the van is available only Saturday. This morning we have no plans except to pray and wait on the Lord for His plans for our morning. A 93 year old Muslim woman walked three miles, then took a bus to our house and invited us to her home for lunch. She made some of the most awesome chicken curry I've ever had. It was so hot and spicy that Tom and I were sweating great drops out of our forearms, as the photos will show. It brought us great laughter because our Indian hosts could not eat the curry as it was too hot for them!! After lunch we had the cell group meeting and there were Christians, Hindus, and Muslims all in the same room. Tom and I prayed for every one of them. Then we were invited to visit and pray over twelve acres of farmland for a local Christian man. We walked through many rows of banana trees and sugar cane. He also chopped open some coconuts so we could drink the liquid inside. It was very tasty and refreshing. Then we went to another house and prayed for an elderly woman. We were out most of the day and it was such a fruitful day for the Lord.

Thursday, Apr. 22nd-

It was cloudy and cooler this morning, but the clouds burned off fast once the sun came up. We spent most of the morning fellowshipping and praying for people as they came by the house. There were two thunderstorms this afternoon. We were able to visit the gypsy camp tonight and what an incredible evening of God's goodness and compassion poured out upon these outcast and rejected people. This camp had been vacated 2 years back as the gypsies tend to do, but now the camp is full again. The original camp leader died a year ago, but five of the original camp members have returned and there was much joy reuniting with them. One was a little girl born crippled and could not walk, but God healed her three years ago. As soon as we got out of the van, she came to me and lifted her arms up toward me and smiled in remembrance of her miracle. Our eyes made contact and our tears of joy flowed. Whenever I see these little children, I am always reminded of my own back home. As we gathered in the tiny one room hut, it quickly filled until there was no room left inside. More gypsies gathered outside to praise with us inside and to hear the Word of God. Then we began to pray one on one for them. Several brought bottles of oil for us to bless so that whenever any of them got sick, they know to anoint with the oil. As we prayed, more and more of them came until nearly the whole camp had come for prayer. Tom and I spent over an hour just praying with them for their needs which were so many, including wives asking for God to do something about their drunken husbands who abuse and beat them, many needs for food, various sicknesses, headaches, stomach problems, sick babies and young children. There are no doctors, no clinics, and no medicines of any kind in these remote mountain villages. Much of their water is contaminated and is a big source of sickness and disease, so they don't drink and get very dehydrated, weak, and many suffer body aches and pains. Finally all of them were prayed for and they thronged our van as we left. Such a stark contrast to when church is finished back home. Every village here is the same. When we come to the meeting house, the people pour out and surround us and want to touch us, shake our hand, and the same when we leave. They are always so eager and hungry for the Lord to touch, bless and heal them. It's very difficult to leave them for another year, because I never know for sure if the Lord will have me to come back here again. I know in my heart I will always want to.

Friday, Apr. 23rd-

It is bright, sunny and warm this morning. George's motorbike is ready. Much work was needed for repairs after seven years of heavy use. He'll pick it up later. Two of my friends from several years back arrived for an unexpected visit; (The former Hindu priest and his wife. I baptized them in the "elephant pond" along with the Muslim man who converted to Christ. He was beheaded while he slept by his father 3 days later). My friends shared how they are living in a different village. When they first came to Christ, they were thrown out of their village along with all their possessions. They lived on the side of the road which is a public toilet under a plastic tarp for 2 years. Now they are the only 2 believers in their new village. They face daily interrogations by the upper caste Hindu religious authorities who want only an excuse to beat them. They are under constant surveillance during Hindu festivals to see if they will attend. They do not, and their answer is always the same: Jesus is the Messiah and I need not to worship Gods made from wood and stone which cannot speak back. They tell us these things with great joy and smiles on their faces. We had wonderful time of fellowship, tea, and prayer. As soon as they left, it was time to go to the dam for the four who wanted to take water baptism. We had planned to do that earlier, but with the dry season just ending and rainy season beginning, there was no water anywhere until the afternoon/evening thunderstorms began to cover the dry lakebed at the dam. The water was a bit dirty from mud and also used by the animals for a water hole. It was just perfect. The mud was very sticky and up to mid-calf level. Tom and I helped Pastor Sharad into the water until it was deep enough, then we went back to the shore and brought out the new believers one by one. When the first person was under the water Pastor Sharad lost his balance in the slippery mud and fell backwards into the water himself. Everyone had a long good laugh and we helped the woman and Pastor Sharad back on their feet. The other 3 candidates went with no further difficulties and soon we were all back on shore celebrating and taking photos. A big lunch soon followed. During the mid afternoon, a very windy, strong thunder-storm with heavy rain and hail came. Of course the power was soon gone, but the storm cooled the air very nicely. Later, with some sadness, we went 1 hour way to our last meeting. But God quickly showed us that He has much of His glory and favor to show us. During that time with these precious ones(who I've known now for 10 years), we were treated to praise/singing by 3 of the men whom I have many photos of: one plays a handmade set of boned drums, one plays an old-fashioned accordion, and one plays a tambourine like no one else I've ever heard. They all sing. Tom set my digital camera to video so we have a little sample of their music to bring home with us. I asked Tom to share the Word because I want to give him the opportunity to teach very short and simple. It's done wonders for his self-esteem and assurance as a young minister of the Word of God. Then we prayed for the room full of people. We stayed awhile for tea/goodies/fellowship. Then several of the people took us to two other houses to pray for their sick - one being the man who last year invited Tom and I to his son's wedding. He was so happy to see us his eyes welled up with tears. Even though we don't know a single word of each other's language, the eyes give much understanding. We then went to the next house and prayed for one sick woman, but soon more people came in and they wanted prayer. Finally we were ready to leave. We were to get up at 4am to head back to Bangalore. But before we got to our van, a man asked if we would go to a distant village at 7am and pray for his brother who was in stage 4 prostate cancer and very sick. (No chemo/radiation available to most) we agreed so off we went.

Saturday, Apr. 24th-

At 5am we got up early after 4 hours of sleep, had tea and packed the van. Soon after, we were off to pray for the sick man. We expected him to be lying nearly lifeless as many are in this advanced stage of cancer. But not this man!. His brother told him we were coming, so he got himself up, washed and dressed very nicely, got out his Bible, was sitting cross-legged on his bed and was waiting for us to come. We found out he was an elderly retired pastor. He wanted to sing a hymn before I shared the Word with him. We read several verses of scripture from John Chapter 11 concerning Lazarus, Acts 10:34 where Peter declared that "God is no respecter of persons", and finally, "Jesus is the same yesterday, today and forever" from Hebrews 13:8. I wanted to build his faith to believe for his life. Then I anointed his head with oil and prayed. It was a moment I shall never forget: how the tears ran down this old pastor's face as God began to touch him. (One day when I too am an old and dying pastor, I would be very happy to have this same experience). In a matter of seconds, his whole countenance changed. He sat more uprightly, smiled, and his face lit up like the morning sunshine. Also, in the same time frame, seven others came quietly into the house, sat on the floor beside his bed, and they too wanted prayer. We were finally ready to walk to the van parked at the end of the street. We turned to look back and saw that all the people were following behind, including the old pastor. I could tell instantly he had been healed by just his appearance and the joy with which he too was walking. We all had a tearful goodbye as we drove away. We got a flat tire but got it fixed, and at last we were on our way back to Bangalore, nearly five hours later than planned. We stopped three times for light snacks and arrived in Bangalore at 4:10pm. The power was out, so it was a good time for a nice refreshing bath. The power came back on so I was checking for any e-mail, and a big thunderstorm came and knocked out the power for another 2½ hours. It finally came back on and I was able to receive very good news and photos of my first grandchild, born back on Tuesday morning the 20th. I knew before leaving America that she was coming probably while I was here. Also good news that British Airways had resumed all flights into and out of London as the Icelandic volcano ash had finally cleared the area. It blew within hours of our departure from London back on Wednesday April 14. So we'll sleep well, knowing we can fly home.

Sunday, Apr. 25th-

Bangalore- a very hazy, warm morning awaits us with all the noises of the big city. All Tom's and my clothes are being washed and today, we're just resting and writing in our journals. It's very unusual to not have the Talavadi Sunday service and then leave, but each year brings its own differences and we are learning not to expect every year to be the same. It was a nice rest day and lots of time to spend with Sharad's family. The power went out 3 times today, but now at 10pm, it's back on.

Monday, Apr. 26th-

Lots of busy street noise to greet us as we awoke in the early morning. There are no plans made for us that we yet know about, so after breakfast, we went into town for more currency exchange and small things needed to repair Sharad's computer. It was lunchtime by the time we returned. The power went out for three hours during the afternoon. Everyone went to bed to "sleep off the heat" with no fans. I'm not used to napping in the afternoon, but today it was ok getting 1 ½ hours of extra sleep. We enjoyed more fellowship, supper, and checked our e-mail before going to bed around 10pm.

Tuesday, Apr. 27th-

I woke up thinking about going home in two more days. As the ministry in Talavadi is finishing for us this year, I began to think about all the things back home to deal with. The day dragged by very slowly and I found it more difficult to basically do nothing but rest and fellowship. The Lord reminded me to just relax and enjoy because once I got home, there won't be such time. Bedtime finally came and I knew this would be our last full night to sleep here this year.

Wednesday, Apr. 28th-

I woke up at 5:45am with excitement because at 6:30am, I was able to check Tom and myself in online and print our boarding passes. This day actually passed quickly and in the early evening, we took Sharad and his family to a Chinese restaurant for our "traditional" last night dinner together. We had a very wonderful time and a very tasty dinner. When we got home, the girls had earlier made a chocolate cake to celebrate Mackenzie's birth back in the States. She was born on Tuesday April 20th, but I couldn't check the e-mail until several days later. She is our first grand child. We enjoyed the small celebration with photos. By then, it was about 9pm. Usually, my last night is a very sad time. Everyone just gets very quiet. But this year, we watched a praise video on Tom's laptop of our home church praise team. It was a very uplifting time for our last night. We went to bed at 10pm.

Thursday, Apr. 29th-

We got up at 2am. We left immediately for the Bangalore airport. It took about an hour and we found the airport already very busy with fellow travelers. It only took us about eight minutes to check our bags and go through security. We had plenty of time left over to reflect upon all we witnessed of the Lord's wonderful work. Finally at 5:45am, we boarded our flight for the 10 hour and 10 minute journey to London. After the first meal was served, we were able to sleep some. Another meal was served about 1 ½ hours before landing in London. It was a very smooth, uneventful, long flight. We went through security in London's Heathrow Airport and went directly to our boarding gate area where we had about two hours to wait for our seven hour flight back to Boston. We ate and slept more on that flight and when we arrived in Boston we could not land immediately because of very high winds at Logan Airport. We had descended from 38,000 feet down to 4,300 feet and we got a beautiful, low altitude view of Boston, South Shore, and coastal areas as we circled twice waiting to land. We were delayed by thirty minutes, but that's not bad considering we had just flown 11,000 miles all on the same day. It didn't take long to clear through immigration, customs and baggage claim. Soon, we were outside in the very cold wind (welcome home!!) waiting for our shuttle van to take us north one hour where Tom's work truck was parked. We got some coffee and sweets and headed for Tom's house in Keene. We arrived there at 10:30pm and I loaded my bags into my truck which I had left there at the beginning of our trip on April 13th. I drove 45 minutes and arrived home at 11:15pm. The whole return trip was an incredible journey of 31 hours and 11,000 miles back through 9 ½ hours of time zone changes. I was very happy to get home and enjoyed a nice hot shower. I finally went to bed at 1:30am. I'm already hopeful that God will make provision to go again next year.

Chapter 15
2011

Tuesday, Apr. 12th, 2011

3pm – It is so wonderful to once again be headed for India. This year's journey is very special because it is now my 20th year of mission trips. Preparations began back in November when I found a great airfare rate in Lufthansa this time. Finances began coming in immediately after I prayed and confirmed by the Holy Spirit that I was to go. Another special event today was the blessing of Dave Wells riding to Logan Airport with Tom and I. Dave was a huge inspiration to me 20 years ago when he took me with him for my first trip in 1991. So now I'm sitting in the boarding area for my 5:05pm flight to Frankfurt, Germany, and then on to Bangalore.

The lines here at the airport were long today, but all went very smoothly. I ate lunch in the same restaurant where Tom and I ate on last year's trip. Now the waiting time is down to 1 ½ hours. That will pass quickly and we'll be on our way. My flight left right on time. We took off toward the southeast and were over the ocean in minutes. We turned northeast and followed the Maine coastline, then Nova Scotia, and on over Newfoundland. A very tasty dinner was served as our plane crossed over St. John's Island at 37,000 feet. A beautiful reddish gold sunset soon followed and the dark of night was upon us as the plane continued on over the icy cold North Atlantic, just south of Greenland. I slept for a little while and when I woke up, we were just over the western coastline of Ireland. It was still dark, but the lights far below sparkled like diamonds. We continued eastward, crossing the Celtic Sea, Wales, southern England, and across the English Channel at Dover. We continued on across Belgium and into Germany. It was getting lighter out and I could see we were over a layer of clouds. As we neared Frankfurt, the plane descended to 15,000 feet and we broke through the clouds. The city lights were beautiful as we passed directly overhead on our way to the airport.

Wednesday, Apr. 13th

At 5:30am, the plane landed two minutes early. Inside the terminal I noticed many new changes since I came through here in 2007. I now found my favorite restaurant is smoke-free. Yippee!! A very good breakfast soon followed. A quick trip through security and now I'm in my boarding gate area. It's 8am and so I still have 3 ½ hours before boarding the plane for Bangalore. But to my great delight, there are all new comfortable chairs to wait in. A trip just made for the King's kid! My flight from Frankfurt to Bangalore was very on time and the view from my window seat was spectacular. After departing from Frankfurt, we flew southeast across Eastern Europe, southwestern Russia, and across the Black Sea. We passed over Eastern Turkey and could easily see the high snow-capped mountains. A more southerly turn brought us over much of Iran where it began to get dark as we passed through more time zones. The GPS map in our plane showed us we also flew along the Persian Gulf, and crossed over the southeast side of Arabia near Dubai. Then we crossed the Arabian Sea, passing over the coastline of India just south of Goa (a very beautiful beach and tourist site.), and 1 ½ hours later, we arrived in Bangalore. After Immigration, Customs, and Baggage Claim was complete, Sharad and Prema were waiting outside for me. We had a wonderful time of reconnecting and fellowship until 2am. The bed felt very nice by then after my 30 hour journey.

Thursday, Apr. 14th-

I woke up quite refreshed after five hours of sleep. We had tea and breakfast, and I sent e-mails home. Then Sharad and I went into the city to just "hang out" together. We found a place to buy vanilla ice cream with almonds- yummie, even at 10 am. It's already 90F. We will not go to Talavadi until Saturday as the house repairs are not quite finished. So I'll have a couple of days to adjust and relax before the long drive to Talavadi and the ministry which will follow. I went to bed at 10:30pm and slept very well.

Friday, Apr. 15th-

I woke up at 5:30am to the noise of busy traffic and some barking dogs. I hadn't planned on being awake so early, but it did give me a great opportunity for prayer and time in the word. Sharad was up soon after and we had tea together out on the balcony, as the early morning sun was rising. It is so nice to be able to go outside so early and it is already 75F. After our tea, I checked my e-mails and was so very blessed to receive much good news from back home in Vermont. Another's victory gave me much reason to rejoice and to be so thankful to God, who always causes us to triumph in Christ. Another blessing was Sharad took me out to breakfast to give Prema a break and the opportunity for her to sleep a little longer. We discovered the need for new brake pads on the van and that was taken care of today. Such repairs are better today than to lose the brakes on the way to Talavadi tomorrow. Today seemed like a lazy day for me – reading the Word, prayer, drinking tea, sitting in the sun, eating, a hot bath and just basically resting and good fellowship. I'll be in bed by 10pm as we'll pack and leave early tomorrow morning.

Saturday, Apr. 16th-

I woke up at 5am and it is already warm. Word came late last night from Talavadi that it had rained heavy for two days and two nights. We were told to come a little later today, so we will leave at 7am instead. So that gave me more time for prayer and the Word. We had thunderstorms in the night, which cooled the air nicely for sleeping and for our long drive this morning. We plan to stop in Mysore for breakfast as we usually do. It's about a short 3 ½ hour drive and gets us out of Bangalore before the traffic gets bad. The traffic turned out to be very heavy, with many slow trucks along the way. It took a lot longer than we thought it would. We stopped twice along the way; once for breakfast and again for lunch. We did stop briefly at Camp Heaven as we neared Talavadi. It was very exciting to see the farmer/caretaker 1 room house fully constructed and painted. Now, as God provides, the electricity can be connected. We also took a few photos and continued onto the house I always stay in. We were warmly greeted by George and Vijaykumar (Pastor Sharad's two workers in the ministry) as we finally arrived at the Talavadi house at 3:30pm – 8 ½ hours from when we started. The repairs are a big improvement and my room was ready. We were all so tired that we took some rest and I slept until 6:15pm. After that much-needed rest, the five of us rejoiced, fellowshipped, shared ministry and concerns, and enjoyed a time of prayer. Then Prema's finest chicken curry came from the kitchen. What a tasty delightful meal we enjoyed. At 10pm we were all ready to sleep for the night. As I went into my room, a huge black spider came scurrying out to greet me on my first night. At first I thought it was a scorpion because he was big. Nevertheless, I trapped him against the wall and he was no match for my sandal as I smashed him thoroughly – end of story and off to bed.

Sunday, Apr. 17th-

A crispy cool morning greeted us here in this mountain village. At 5am, the Muslims call to prayer woke up the whole village as it always does, when broadcast by powerful loudspeakers at the nearby mosque. The crows were screaming loudly as well, and the roosters were crowing too. It is truly a rural village and such a joy to be back here.

After tea with Sharad and a fresh hot bath, I'm very ready for the church service which will begin at 9:30am. Right now, I am in my room and the sounds of many happy children fill the house as they arrive for Sunday school. Many of them I have known since their birth and how much they have grown in age and their love for Jesus.

The adult service started a half hour after and it was so good to see so many familiar faces once again. It was like a love reunion with Jesus. These people live a very hard life and it was such a joy to bring them a reminder of God's passionate love and care for them. When prayer time came, God manifested His love for them in many ways as we all prayed together for each other. One after another, one could see hope return on their faces. We prayed for body aches and pains to the return of drunken gambling husbands who had run away from their wives and children. The most touching moment was praying for a young one year old girl with very serious brain damage. She could do nothing and could not utter a sound, but after prayer, she began to make noises and move around. Her mother was so touched with joy, her head covering was soaking wet with her tears. It was a moment suspended in time as everyone watched and waited to see what God would do, if anything. Many of the people stayed for tea and fellowship after the meeting and I was invited for dinner on Wednesday at the Muslim woman's house where last year Tom and I had the really hot, spicy chicken curry. As far as I know, we do not have any other meetings scheduled, but different people come to the house to visit and for prayer. It's already 5pm and getting dark as a large thunderstorm approaches. The temperature reached 103F and very humid for here in the mountains. George and Vijaykumar came back later after supper and all five of us stayed up until almost 11pm discussing today's meeting and much good fellowship around the famous red table.

Monday, Apr. 18th-

It is another warm humid morning at 6:15am. All the usual early morning birds are chirping and singing unto the Lord as the sun is rising like a large orange ball over the peaks of the Nilgiri Mountains. We have no plans for the day except to pray and wait on the Lord. At 10:30am two women came here for prayer. One had come by last year and received prayer for a serious tooth infection which had spread into her sinuses and eyes. She had gone to three distant hospitals by bus, but they could not help her. She told us this morning that she received healing in only three days after praying for her. She brought her friend by for prayer also today. Her friend had been severely beaten by her husband only yesterday. Her injuries included a blackened, swollen face, an upper left arm bone fracture, and a dislocated shoulder. It is heartbreaking to know there are no laws enforced to protect women from such violence and abuse. I've seen it here first hand every year for ten years. Many are beaten by their husbands simply because they are Christians and their husbands are not, so that behavior is even more permissible and widely accepted among the villagers.

After we prayed for these two, we all had some tea together and at noon they rode the bus back to their village. Then the power went out for four hours, so it got pretty hot and stuffy inside. At 5pm we drove one hour to the gypsy camp. I've been going there mostly every year as well. Except for three old women, the others are all quite new to the camp. The little house we met in quickly filled with children and adults. George and Vijaykumar have a cell group here which meets every Monday night at 6pm. There were many prayer needs, but one stood out to me. One of the older women had a 15 year old daughter which I've known since she was five and I have photos of her with the other children. Last fall, she got sick from some sort of fever and she died three days later. Because of the great distance to the nearest hospital and no money to pay to take her, she died. Her mother was so distraught and angry at God that she threw away her bible and went into an uncontrollable rage for a week. But tonight she raised her arms and finally gave God all her pain and anguish and re-dedicated her life to Jesus. God was so pleased with her return to Him. He filled her with His peace, restored her faith and hope in him, and forgave her because at the time she blamed God she did not know what she was doing. When we left, all the people followed us outside to the van, touching us and shaking our hands. They didn't want us to leave. It was very hard to see them all standing and watching us drive away. It's times like this that remind me of why I am so compelled to return each year. I know most people do not understand me, but they have not seen, heard, or touched some of the most rejected and unknown people in the world as I have, and tonight as I prepare to go to bed, I am so very thankful to God for sharing His precious gems with me.

Tuesday, Apr. 19th-

I woke up at 4am and stayed awake. No one else was up yet. It was a great time for prayer and the Word. At 6:15am, Pastor Sharad was up and we had our tea together at the red table. It was already warm and humid. The power went out at 9am (which has been the same every day since I arrived in Talavadi on Saturday.)

Sharad and I had the opportunity to ride for one hour to the nearest city with internet service at a cybershop, spent another hour waiting for a computer to be available to check/send e-mails only to find the computer filled with so many viruses that the e-mail service would not function, so then we drove another hour back to the house. That was quite a disappointment, but former missionaries had no such luxuries to distract them from their mission. After lunch, heavy rain and wind came. We had a cell group meeting scheduled in the forest village only 15 kilometers away, but it took more than on hour to go there in the rain. Along the way, we drove through two washouts and several flooded areas of the road. When we arrived, the house was already filled with eager excited people to welcome us. This is the village where ten years back, a young boy was healed. At that time, he was born crippled and could not walk. He used his hands to drag his body around from place to place. I see him every year and last year, when he turned 18 years, he was tending his father's sheep. This year, he is of much help in even more responsibilities on his father's farm. He is still very much healed as though he had never been born with such an infirmity. There were many prayer needs and God was so lovingly kind and compassionate to these forest villagers. When we were ready to leave, someone came to the house and asked us to come to another house to pray. When we walked there in the rain, we found that house filled with people, not just one or two. So we joyfully prayed for each one of them. Then we went to a third house to pray for one man who could not be moved. Finally, we departed and came by George's house where a very nice hot supper had been prepared for us. So by the time we got back to our house, it was 10:30pm. We had tea and went to bed.

Wednesday, Apr. 20th-

Today, back home in Vermont, it is my granddaughter's first birthday. She was born to our son while I was here last year. Sometimes, when such family treasures happen, it's sad to not be able to be home for those times. But my trips are scheduled months before, and plans like that cannot be changed. So today I will still remember Mackenzie.

From 9am until 1pm, I am doing a Pastors' Seminar here at the house. We are hopeful at least twelve to fifteen pastors and their wives will attend. Once again, it will get pretty toasty in the house. I have forty more minutes to review my teaching material and then we begin. It is now 5:30pm. How fast the day went by!! Pastors began arriving on buses from their respective areas and the final count was eleven and no wives. But we considered it was a good response to the invitations. The meeting went very well and after ending with communion and prayer, I was asked to come back in six months to do another seminar. I told them it would be in one year if God provides for me to be here again next year.

Then we went to the Muslim woman's house for lunch where Tom and I had the really hot chicken curry last year. She lessened the spice level so Pastor Sharad could eat it. Then we had a very nice time of fellowship and prayer. Wow! I nearly forgot a miracle! Too much curry, I guess. I was then taken to a thatched hut to pray for a baby who would not sleep. Outside the hut, I made the comment, "She will be starting today." As I walked into the hut to pray, the baby immediately went to sleep. The grandmother said, "No need to pray. Just you being here put the baby to sleep." So that was really neat. We came back to the house with very full bellies as the old woman jokingly gave me a double portion since Tom wasn't here this time.

I think tonight we are not going out anywhere so supper may be around 8:30pm. It was and a good night's sleep will be very welcome.

Thursday, Apr. 21st-

Another beautiful sunny morning has begun. These nice days are as regular as breathing. It's warm and humid and the Nilgiri Mountains are hazy. Afternoon thunderstorms are becoming more numerous as the summer rainy season draws nearer. Counting today, I have only four days remaining in Talavadi. How fast the time is slipping away. I will be back home in Vermont in one week. After tea and breakfast, Sharad and I went again to the cybershop in the distant city. This time there was no waiting and the computer was working perfectly, so e-mails were able to be sent. By the time we returned to Talavadi, it was midday and we all had lunch at George's mom's house. During lunch, I found out more about the woman who was beaten so badly by her husband. He had taken a rock and not only broken her left arm, dislocated her shoulder, but also broke her collar bone. I saw the x-ray from the Mysore Hospital. That is the closest hospital to Talavadi and nearly a three hour drive. She is still in a lot of pain, but her face looks better today, and we are trusting the Lord for her complete recovery. After lunch we came back to our house for a 45 minute rest. We then drove 1 ½ hours to a new cell group in a far away village. It was good to see how much work by George and Vijay kumar has been invested in evangelism. There were quite a few children as well at this meeting. After sharing the Word, I prayed for all the people, including a woman who was deaf in one ear after a severe beating by her husband a few months back. After the meeting, we were invited to stay for supper. That was a nice blessing since the ride home was so long. When we returned, one of Prema's sisters stopped by. Back in 2007, I had been taken to her flat in Mysore to pray for her. She had ovarian cancer and nothing else could be done for her, so she was released by the Mysore Hospital. There were two other women at the same time with her who refused prayer – they both died and she was completely healed, and to this day, four years later, she remains cancer free. I call these people God's Miracle Hall of Famers because in each village, there are those who still live because they were healed and openly testify to others. After a late evening of visiting and tea, I went to bed at 11pm. We all got woke up by a very heavy thunderstorm. It seemed to last for a couple of hours. Just after going back to sleep, I was awakened again by something which fell on my head in the dark. I grabbed my flashlight and found that a rat had dropped a rice ball he had been eating on the top of the wall above my head. He didn't come in the room, but he did lose his supper.

Friday, Apr. 22nd-

I woke up at 5:45 for the day, so I didn't get many hours of sleep. I'll just trust god to sustain me very nicely. It's still cloudy and humid. I was told this morning that Sharad wants to take me into the higher peaks of the Nilgiri Mountains today, since we have only one meeting this evening. Our driver is supposed to be here at 8 am, but he's been a little late several times. Going further into the mountains will be refreshing and cooler at elevations of seven to eight thousand feet. Here in Talavadi we are just under six thousand feet above sea level. We all had tea, hot baths, a light breakfast, and now we're waiting for the driver to come for us. What a wonderful fun day with George, Vijay kumar, Sharad and myself, plus our driver. Prema stayed here at the house with her sister who stayed over night last night. The mountain tops were still in the clouds when we left Talavadi and headed east. About 45 minutes later, we were steadily climbing higher. We stopped for tea and continued on. The clouds began to lift and the view was spectacular especially going down the other side of the mountains. There were 27 hairpin turns going down into the deep valley and plains. We drove into quite a large city where we went to a huge dam. George, VJ and I climbed concrete steps all the way to the top of the dam where we could take lots of photos of the lake and surrounding mountains. That was some very good exercise. We stopped for lunch on the way back, and by the time we got back to the mountains, the summits were all in the clear. We stopped several more times for photos, and again on the summit. It was breezy and much cooler than the valley floor below. We got back to the Talavadi house around 4pm where we enjoyed a nice rest from our long seven hour journey. After our rest, we then drove nearly 45 minutes away to the Friday night cell group. It was, once again, like a warm homecoming of sorts for me. This meeting was in the village where several years back a man's son had committed suicide. It was then when he gave me a lamb. Last year when I was here with Tom, he invited both of us to his other son's wedding. Tonight, I had the great joy of seeing this father once again. We embraced and it was like only yesterday that I was here last. After the cell group meeting was finished, Ram, (pronounced rahm) invited us to his house for tea and sweets. I had the joy of praying for his wife and himself and then his two daughters-in law, one of which, is four months pregnant. It was her wedding Tom and I attended last year. The whole family is hoping for a son. We drove home in some light rain, had supper, more good fellowship and I went to bed around 10pm.

Saturday, Apr. 23rd-

I woke up a little later this morning to find it still cloudy and cool. But by the time we finished breakfast, the sun was shining brightly. We went to Camp Heaven for a couple of hours of prayer for the land and it's provisions. Then George, Vijaykumar and I had a prayer walk seven times around the perimeter of the property. Each time we had made one complete circle, the Lord showed me to place a stone beside the well. On each walk around the property, The Lord showed me that the land adjoining Camp Heaven would be abundantly blessed and prosperous, and producing fruitful crops because of the overflow of anointing and blessing on the land of Camp Heaven. It became more and more exciting each time around. On the sixth time, the Lord showed me a reddish colored stone to place with the other five stones. Then after the seventh time around, He showed me a shiny white quartz stone to place on the top of the other six stones. Then He showed me why as best as I can describe we walked seven times around the land as the Israelites did around the city of Jericho. Just as the city walls fell, and the enemy was defeated, so were all the spiritual curses and hindrances broken over the land of Camp Heaven. Each of the first five stones represented a spiritual giant defeated as David also had five stones: one for Goliath and one for each of his brothers if needed. The reddish stone represented Jesus as the Rose of Sharon that all things are subject to Him now on this land, and the white stone represented His righteousness which has now been established on Camp Heaven. The stones were placed at the well to illustrate that just as the water from the well will bring natural sustenance for the crops, and refreshment for the thirsty, there is another "well" there which will be exactly like the river flowing from the temple in Ezekiel's vision in Ezekiel Chapter 47:1-12. So it was a very exciting and encouraging time of prayer and the things God revealed to us. We came home around 1:30pm for lunch, fellowship, and rest time.

At 5pm we went out again, this time to Vijaykumar's for a cell group meeting. I had mentioned to Pastor Sharad that the Scriptures I brought were very different from what I usually have. They came from James 4:7-8, dealing with submitting to God and resisting the devil. At that meeting, there was a strong and noticeable resistance to this word. There was an immediate confusion which came over George as he read the verses in the local language first. The children became very noisy and disruptive, a man quickly left the meeting, and I could literally feel the pressure to not talk about these verses. But I continued until finished, including prayer for all who came. As I finished praying, some words came to me: "There's no one in authority," "witchcraft," "occult". I asked Pastor Sharad about these words while we were driving home. Then he explained to me some very helpful background information about this village and particularly the specific house we held the meeting in. The villages are mostly Hindu and serve many other gods. They also have been involved with invoking curses upon each other over land and property disputes. This family in particular, has a history of being involved in such activity. They are not yet born again believers. They are Presbyterians and believe very similar to Catholicism, but not the worship of Mary. They also endorse many of the Hindu traditions. Thus, as the Lord gave the first words to me: "There's no one in authority" meaning there was no believer to take dominion over the demonic spiritual activity we encountered. As concerning "witchcraft" and "occult" this present house owner has been and openly is involved with speaking curses upon the neighbors over water usage and property disputes. It is no small wonder why there was so much resistance to submitting to God's authority through Jesus Christ as I had been teaching. What a wonderful learning experience and to see how faithful God is to give just the most perfect Scripture for this meeting!! He is always so good, and always so right. And then, just for the grand finale of the evening, as we were finishing our supper, a rat decided he would come into the kitchen in search of any food scraps. He was very foolish to try such a thing with all the house lights on. George spotted him and like a flash, he was beating him with a broom. All the while our driver from Bangalore had arrived and was sleeping on the floor. When he was awakened by all the commotion, he got very afraid, being from the city and coming here where these things are very common. Vijaykumar tried to reassure this driver by telling him he need not worry about a rat, as they had killed a cobra in my room two weeks before I came here. The driver found no comfort in those words and I don't know how well he slept after that.

Sunday, Apr. 24th-

I woke up early today at 5:45. It is cool and cloudy again. Praise the Lord – our driver is still here!! We didn't know if he would flee in fear in the night and leave us stuck in Talavadi. We will be leaving early on Monday morning, so I am down to the last two meetings – this morning's Sunday service and one final cell group meeting later this evening. I can hear the happy sounds of many children coming in for Sunday school, so we will be starting very soon. What a glorious and wonderful time we all had. After the children's church was finished, the adults began arriving by bus from their respective villages. Soon, the small hall was filled, many here from the distant gypsy camp. After much praise and worship and the Word, it was time to pray for all the people. Many things are very common and some heartbreaking. One such case was a young 15 year old gypsy girl forced by her parents to marry at the age of fourteen years. After a year of rape and other cruelties, he has left her for another young girl. She came trusting and believing that if we prayed, God would make everything turn out ok and return her husband to her. What wonderful and powerful faith she has! I so much admire her for that. That kind of faith could and would turn this world upside down. *Testimony concerning the sleeping baby back on Wednesday – the grandmother says today that the baby has been sleeping regularly since Wednesday.

We've enjoyed my last lunch in Talavadi and now we're resting for tonight's cell group meeting at 6pm. The last meeting was held at George's mom's house and the place was full up. Again, so many prayer needs and God was so loving and kind to all of these dear ones. Sick children, broken marriages, praying God's blessing upon 2 new babies, and then I was taken to another close by house to pray for a demon possessed young boy of 16 years old. His parents didn't know what to do for him. Every night around midnight, he would wake up screaming and run from the house into the forest where he roamed and screamed the rest of the night. His eyes were open very wide and darting from side to side and he would not look at me. So I just simply addressed an unclean spirit to come out of him. The boy immediately was transformed before our very eyes. He looked as though he were melting as he quivered slightly and began to relax. You could see how all that tenseness and fear left him. His eyes became normal, he smiled, and then became very friendly. What a blessing to see such a young man's life so quickly restored. He is still in school and had run away often from his classroom. Not any more. Praise the Lord. Then we all stayed for supper and went to bed late. We are going to get up around 4am for packing and tea and depart for Bangalore at 5am.

Monday April 25th

I was so excited about the beginning of my long journey home that I woke up early and was up at 3:35am. It was cloudy and quite cool. I had plenty of time for last minute packing and morning devotional time, and the tea as we all were up already. We had some prayer time together and we left Talavadi at 5:05am. It was still pitch dark as we headed out. It was good to leave early because there was hardly any traffic except for a few trucks. We arrived in Mysore at 7:50am and had a nice buffet breakfast at the hotel restaurant which we always stop at going and coming. The traffic steadily got heavier as we left. Mysore is a very large city which attracts tourists from all over the world to visit it's famous Mysore palace. Our driver skillfully navigated us through and we got into the outer part of Bangalore by 10:30am, but it took until 11:45am to actually reach Sharad's Bangalore apartment. All his daughters were so happy to see their mom and dad. We rested awhile, checked e-mail and had a nice lunch. Pastor Sharad was very tired from the long road trip and he went to bed for a few hours. I answered my e-mails and had some computer difficulties in sending them so I'll try again tomorrow. I had a refreshing hot bath and just rested/relaxed the rest of the afternoon and evening. Sharad and I had tea after he got up from his nap. At around 8pm as we were getting ready for supper, the daily power outage occurred so we had a cozy candlelight supper. The power came back on around 9 so it gave the ceiling fans time to re-cool the rooms for sleeping. By 10pm I was ready for that.

Tuesday April 26th

I woke up at 5:45am to a warm, humid Bangalore morning. There must have been some mosquitoes in my room as I had a few bites, but no big deal - we have mosquitoes in Vermont too. No one is up yet as I'm writing, but I know Sharad will be up very soon. He is much like me in that regard – we are both early morning people. Last night we all discussed where we might like to go out for our annual traditional last night supper together. The girls all decided on Domino's Pizza so I guess that's where we'll be later. In the meantime, I'm just going to enjoy my last two days here as I leave for the airport tomorrow evening. I've got lots of clothes to be washed, rewrite and send the failed e-mails from yesterday, go into town and get the tea for Mrs. Holloway to bring home with me, and just see how the day unfolds. Grace will probably go with me as we always go to a café coffee house on my last day here. Well it didn't take long for a small change of plans. Grace had a special meeting with some of her teaching staff from Nirikshea School and she was gone most of the day, so I took Pastor Sharad in her place. We enjoyed our noisy ride in the 3-wheeler rickshaw to the café coffee shop about 3 ½ miles from here. We both had their famous Aztec International coffee and a large piece of chocolate cake covered in hot chocolate syrup. That was so good and on the way back to the house, we both realized what a caffeine buzz we got. Prema wondered what happened to us. We had a light lunch around 2pm and had a lazy restful afternoon. At around 7:30pm, our driver came and drove us all to Domino's Pizza. We all had a fun time together and the pizza and the garlic bread was awesome! We brought lots of the leftovers home and we'll have the garlic bread for breakfast instead of toast. I stayed up until 11pm and went to bed with a joy-filled heart and a pizza-filled belly.

Wednesday April 27th

I woke up at 5:45am to the usual sounds of a big city. It's warm and humid as I sit by the window writing in this journal. Grace has rescheduled some other meetings until later so we can go to the coffee shop. I'm very sure I'll have what I had yesterday. It's time to check e-mails as there are several things going on back home in Vermont that I need to stay aware of. Grace and I got back around 2:30pm after coffee and some shopping. I tried to sleep for a little while since it's going to be a very long ride night, but that didn't work. I'm getting very excited now about going home. I had an earlier supper and a hot bath, packed all my stuff and we left for the airport at 9:45pm. It was good we left a few minutes early as there was still a lot of traffic, construction and detours. We got to the airport at 11:10 and I am now sitting in a café, having checked in and gone through security. There are many people flying out tonight, so it took a bit longer than usual, but everything went smoothly. We will be able to board the flight for Frankfurt, Germany in about an hour, so now it's a nice quiet wait. I should be able to get some sleep on the plane since it's a ten hour flight. We left Bangalore right on time with a full flight. No empty seats. But mine way in the back was most welcoming. I have a five hour layover in Frankfurt, so no need to hurry. I did get a few hours of uninterrupted sleep, but survived nicely. Two excellent meals were served as well. I also noticed from the onboard flight tracker that we took a much more northeasterly course than the other times I've taken this flight. We flew nearly north for all of India and not over the Arabian Sea. We stayed inland and flew over Iran and Azerbaijan, also passing over the Caspian Sea instead of the Baltic Sea. We then turned a bit northwest, crossing over southwest Russia (Ukraine) and on into Eastern Europe. As we were crossing over Czechoslovakia, I saw many familiar cities from the four missions trips there in the 1990's. We continued westward across Germany and arrived in Frankfurt right on time.

Thursday April 28th

It's cloudy and cool here in Frankfurt Germany, but the air feels refreshing after leaving 103F Bangalore. It was a little bumpy descending through three layers of clouds and the bright sunshine of high altitude flying quickly disappeared. In the airport, I've had a nice thirty minute walk to my gate area instead of taking a shuttle train. The exercise felt good after sitting for so long. Security was quick with no lines, and now I'm in my boarding area. I do still have a three hour wait, but better early than late. It's neat to know I'll be in Boston this afternoon and home by 6:45pm. My flight left exactly on time and I was a bit disappointed to see that it was cloudy all the way to Boston. So I used the opportunity to sleep a few more hours. When I arrived in Boston, I felt reasonably rested and really enjoyed my time with Tom as we drove to Chester. I was so happy to see baby leaves on the trees and the snow was all gone!!!

I arrived home in Chester at 7:05pm, all the clothing in my suitcase went into the washing machine, I went into the nice hot shower, then Faith and I had a nice light supper together and I stayed up until 10pm sharing many of the things that had happened here while I was in India, and the things which happened in India. And, as always is the case, the Lord really showed His great mercy and compassion over and over again on this journey of miracles.